BUILDING RELATIONSHIPS, YIELDING RESULTS

HOW SUPERINTENDENTS CAN WORK WITH SCHOOL BOARDS TO CREATE PRODUCTIVE TEAMS

Julie L. Hackett

Harvard Education Press
Cambridge, Massachusetts

Library of Congress Control Number 2014959080
Paperback ISBN 978-1-61250-806-1
Library Edition ISBN 978-1-61250-807-8

Published by Harvard Education Press,
an imprint of the Harvard Education Publishing Group

Harvard Education Press
8 Story Street
Cambridge, MA 02138

Cover Design: Wilcox Design
Cover Image: © iStock.com/Jorgenmac
The typefaces used in this book are Dante and Steagal

CONTENTS

INTRODUCTION

Transforming Superintendent and School Board Relationships

TRIALS, TRIBULATIONS, AND TRIUMPHS IN THE TAUNTON PUBLIC SCHOOLS

At a heated school board meeting in Taunton, Massachusetts, in July 2007, a veteran school board member argued with the superintendent of schools about his proposal to lay off two school nurses. Embroiled in an ongoing and bitter battle with the superintendent, the board member was determined to keep school nursing services intact. As tensions mounted on this hot summer day, the unhappy school board member expressed frustration with the proposal and publicly berated the superintendent. One of his colleagues, who happens to be Jewish and the sole supporter of the former superintendent, interrupted the school board member telling him not to raise his voice and to act more professionally. To everyone's shock, the agitated school board member responded sharply, "Yes, heil Hitler. Sieg heil."[1]

Too stunned to comment, the mayor, the superintendent, and the school board let the matter go unresolved. Accounts of the incident quickly began to circulate in the media, and city officials and members of the Jewish community publicly expressed their disappointment at the school board member's offensive remarks. The Anti-Defamation League demanded a public apology calling the unfortunate turn of events a "teachable moment," city officials called for his ouster, and the mayor issued a statement declaring that "every public official . . . should conduct themselves in a professional manner, whether they're addressing another committee member or anyone from the public."[2] In the end, the school board member chose not to resign, but he later asked for forgiveness in a written public statement, abandoning his intent to run for the school board in a subsequent term.

Amidst all this turmoil and only days after the heated exchange, the same school board offered me the position of assistant superintendent. I remember feeling a palpable tension during my interview, but undeterred both out of curiosity and necessity (I was relocating to Massachusetts from another state, and I needed a job), I soon learned that this was not the only issue between the superintendent and the school board. According to certain board members, the superintendent had been abruptly appointed to his post, and the background check process was bypassed due to political pressure that was either real or perceived. Those who did not agree with his hiring harbored deep resentment about the manner in which the superintendent had been appointed to his position, which worsened their relationship with the superintendent and created a growing rift among school board members.

Soon, unfortunate and unflattering headlines seemed to proliferate in the media. School board meetings that board members already considered to be highly dysfunctional became even more so, and the public regarded the antics that occurred at bimonthly meetings (in the words of one teacher) as "the best show in town." Employees still tell tales of popping popcorn and hosting get-togethers for their in-town and out-of-town friends and colleagues. Together, they watched the televised school board meetings on their big screens, and while the strained superintendent–school board relations did little to help the school system or its children, these meetings apparently made for some riveting reality television.

Seven years later, I find myself in my sixth year as superintendent of schools in this same district—a school community that I have grown to love. I am thankful that our relationships today look vastly different than in previous years, which is a credit to the school board, the educators, and the citizens in Taunton who want more for our schools and children. The original school board is still largely intact with all but two of our current school board members having served in 2007, making our transformation all the more meaningful.

I am happy to say that as I write this, school board member interactions and superintendent–school board relationships are now recognized as highly functional and consistently focused on students. Most important, as a result of these productive relationships, student achievement and outcomes have dramatically improved, but this transformation did not occur by accident. In 2009, after I was appointed superintendent, I began to further develop a set of strategies to build collaborative and high-functioning teams and improve student outcomes. Some of these strategies came from my work in various school systems in Maine and Massachusetts. In 2010, educators in other communities started to notice the positive changes in our school system, inviting me to speak more widely at superintendent and school board conferences to share these ideas. Others suggested I compile these strategies in a published work, and as a result, you have this book in your hands today.

I have spent close to fifteen years as a school and central office administrator serving students in all grade spans; in rural, suburban, and urban areas; and in both socioeconomically disadvantaged and affluent school systems. It has been said that to develop extraordinary expertise in a given area, a person has to invest at least ten thousand hours of her time.[3] During my decade and a half as a central office leader, I have been a close observer of superintendent and school board relationships, and I have participated in more formal and informal school board meetings than I can count. Throughout my life's work, I think it is fair to say that I have logged far more than ten thousand hours observing superintendent–school board relationships.

While I am not convinced that time alone makes one an expert, I have been drawn to the complex interactions that exist between the superintendent and school board since my early days as a school leader. I have learned the most by observing superintendents with wonderful ideas and good intentions who struggled to build high-functioning teams, engaging school board members in meaningful ways. Most troubling to me has been the impact that these poor superintendent–school board relations have on those *not* directly involved, and it is heartbreaking to see how the tensions can lead to the inertia of an entire school community. Through the years, I have watched what happens to school systems when their highly capable school leaders and school boards become embroiled in controversy over relatively minor matters, and the idealist in me has always believed that there must be a better way.

That better way was out of reach for me when I first became superintendent because relationship-building resources for those in school leadership positions have always been scarce. It is not surprising that so many superintendent–school board teams are marked by discord given the lack of information; some superintendents have been trained to inundate school boards with trivial distractions to keep them preoccupied, or to actively ignore or spend as little time as possible with school boards, hoping they will be left alone to do what they can to help students achieve more. As you will read, my philosophy is different.

I believe the best way for superintendents to bring about sustainable school transformation is to build relationships with school boards through close collaboration on engaging and meaningful work that matters most to children. This philosophy is developed in the two primary sections of this book: in the first five chapters, I share a system you, as superintendent, can use to build effective relationships with your school board; and the last four chapters are devoted to the strategies that you need to practice consistently to achieve successful twenty-first century school reform.

In chapter 1, I frame the problem with educational reform today and how it affects our children. In chapters 2 through 5, I share familiar strategies that superintendents can use, including the entry process, norms and beliefs protocols, strategic planning, and goal setting, but unlike in other works, I situate these processes in the context of relationship building. These strategies are meant to be iterative, repeated, and revisited in order to foster better communication and build productive teams. New superintendents can benefit from executing the pre-entry strategy (chapter 2) prior to establishing norms and beliefs protocols (chapter 3), a strategic plan (chapter 4), and a set of inclusive goals with their school board (chapter 5). Experienced superintendents who want to establish or re-establish productive relationships with their boards can start with a re-entry plan (chapter 2), and then pick up from among the strategies that are either new for the district or those that could benefit school board members, such as the community input team process (chapter 6). In chapters 6 through 9, I focus on how you can deal with the challenging issues of race and changing demographics, how to show care and concern for the community, and how to communicate effectively, sustaining the relationships that you have worked so hard to build. These chapters emphasize how the different approaches can help you ready yourself for the work ahead and forge stronger bonds with members of your school board and school community.

Each chapter begins with an "at-a-glance" reference designed to give you a glimpse of the action steps needed to effectively implement the technique being discussed. Since there is a shortage of relationship-building "how to" books for school leaders, wherever possible, I have included a detailed breakdown of the steps involved in a particular relationship-building strategy, along with artifacts and authentic examples that help bring those strategies to life. In the early chapters, you will read about a "rock star" reformer who was quickly shown the door by his school board, and then you will read about Andrés Alonso, the former superintendent of the Baltimore Public Schools, who made sweeping changes in an urban school system and managed to keep his school board relationships intact. It is my hope that the structure of this book provides you with a framework that you can use to easily replicate some of these ideas to build better superintendent–school board relationships that make a lasting difference for your students.

Finally, a note on usage. I have written this book primarily as a resource for superintendents, including aspiring, new, and veteran leaders. For convenience, I use the term *you* to refer to this audience; however, I believe this book can also be a resource for school board members, policy makers, and other educators and leaders who are looking for ways to bring about more sustainable school reform. This book is for politicians, parents, teachers, administrators, college professors, school board members, state board of education members, state officials, and organizations promoting school reform—all those who have a vested interest in creating better schools for our children.

THE IMPORTANCE OF CONTEXT IN BUILDING RELATIONSHIPS

The relationship-building strategies shared in this book have proven effective in small- and mid-sized urban school systems in Maine and Massachusetts, but they are also applicable and, in my view desperately needed, in larger urban school systems across the nation. Those "great city schools" like Boston, Miami-Dade, and Los Angeles could all benefit from the relationship-building strategies that could begin to transform a skeptical public's opinion that large urban school systems are nothing more than bureaucratic, depersonalized waste lands that are failing our children. As Cronin says, "It has become fashionable to label public schools a monolithic monopoly, impervious to change or new direction," and he explains further that parental values are often exercised when a choice is made to "'exit' from a school system."[4] If you ask parents what they really want from their child's school, most will say this: "I want to know that my child is in a safe and joyful learning environment, where they are respected, valued, and loved." The relationship-building strategies in this book help create those conditions, and they can benefit urban school districts both large and small.

By the same token, the strategies in this book are in no way intended to be a relationship-building formula that works the same way in every community. The best way to make use of the ideas offered in this work is to reflect on these strategies and determine what approach might work best for you in your situation with your unique assemblage of school board members. Effective leaders hold deep understandings of their own strengths and limitations, as well as an appreciation for the context and the people with whom they work. They know intuitively that a "one size fits all" approach seldom works in the classroom, in a school, or across a system of schools. Superintendents who tailor strategies to honor and respect the community they lead are more successful school leaders. Simply put, what works in Taunton, Massachusetts, will not necessarily work in Mobile, Alabama; Detroit, Michigan; or Poughkeepsie, New York, so I encourage you to customize the relationship-building techniques in this book to best meet the particular needs of your school community.

Since much of this book centers on my work with a school board in an urban school district in Taunton, Massachusetts, it is fitting for me to share with you some of the city's background and history. No doubt you will see similarities and differences with your own community. In many respects Taunton mirrors demographic trends that are being experienced in cities and towns across the country: increasing numbers of students living in poverty, an influx of English language learners, and more children at-risk for dropping out of school. Schools throughout the nation are also experiencing decreasing public support and inadequate funding to address the growing needs of their students. In my mind, these trends make the relationship-building strategies among leaders even more important given their potential for enhancing problem solving, encouraging community buy-in for solutions, and acquiring more resources and support.

Taunton is a family-oriented community composed of individuals who are inclined to value history, politics, and tradition. Although it is the largest city in Massachusetts in terms of square mileage, with a population of approximately fifty-six thousand,[5] a preferred expression among locals is "Taunton's more like a small town than a big city." Loosely translated, this means that Tauntonians take pride in their city, know their neighbors, and treat one another like family. In the same way a brother or sister at once incites and inspires, Tauntonians "duke it out" like any other citizen when they get upset, yet no matter how mercurial their tempers may be, they are also quick to come to the rescue of a neighbor during times of hardship and tragedy.

Tauntonians possess a strong sense of community, but they are also fiercely independent, which can be traced back to colonial days. On March 3, 1639, the City of Taunton was founded by Elizabeth Poole (anglicized later to Pole), an English settler in the Plymouth colonies, and the first woman known to have founded a town in the Americas.[6] Robert Treat Paine, a Taunton lawyer, the first attorney general in Massachusetts, and the Associate Justice of the Massachusetts Supreme Judicial Court, signed the Declaration of Independence, which was approved by Congress on July 4, 1776.[7] The Taunton Public School system was established in 1838,[8] and I now have the honor and privilege of being the first female superintendent in the city's history. The Mayor of Taunton serves as an ex officio member of the school board, along with eight additional school board members, all of whom face re-election every two years in accordance with the city charter. This means that the possibility exists for the superintendent to work with a brand new school board and mayor every two years.

Taunton struggles socioeconomically, and it is considered one of nearly two dozen "Gateway Cities," a title given by the Massachusetts state legislature to once-prosperous, mid-sized urban centers with low median household incomes and low educational attainment. In Taunton, the median household income falls approximately $10,000 behind the state average, and 19 percent of its residents hold a bachelor's degree or higher compared to the state average of 39 percent. The school district is recognized as one of twenty-four urban school systems in the Commonwealth of Massachusetts.[9]

There are approximately eight thousand two hundred students and one thousand two hundred fifty staff members from diverse socioeconomic and cultural backgrounds in the Taunton Public Schools. Taunton High School, which now houses students in grades 8–12, is the fifth largest high school in the state behind Boston, New Bedford, Springfield, and Worcester, Massachusetts.[10] More than half of the students in the school system qualify for free and reduced lunch, with more than 80 percent of students in some schools living in poverty. Students hail from twenty-eight countries, and approximately twenty-three languages are spoken in the district, including: Cape Verdean Creole, Spanish, Mandarin, Bulgarian, Pashto, Urdu, and Haitian Creole.

Roughly 70 percent of Taunton's students are Caucasian, and 30 percent are students of color although this statistic has been in question. According to Halter, "Official Census figures have not been of use in defining the Cape Verdean immigrant population, so it is unclear whether census data accurately reflect the Afro-Portuguese population who settled in southeast Massachusetts and self-identify as white."[11] Today, Taunton has one of the largest populations of Portuguese in Massachusetts, many of whom are Cape Verdean.[12] Cape Verde is an archipelago off the coast of West Africa near Senegal that was colonized by

Portugal in the fifteenth century. The Cape Verdeans voluntarily made their way across the Atlantic to America, where their survival depended on their assimilation with Caucasians. Historical and institutionalized racism forced Cape Verdeans to disregard their African ancestry and identify as white in order to survive. As a result, Cape Verdeans have come to be known as "invisible people" or a "people without a race."[13] Although the data may not accurately reflect our student demographics, the Afro-Portuguese community remains an important part of Taunton's culture, and their diversity is reflected in our public schools.

AGAINST THE GRAIN REFORM

School reformers today will probably tell you that the needs of our students are so great, so urgent, and public education is failing so miserably that they cannot afford to waste a second on school board relationship building. *This* school reformer says that is nonsense. A first-generation college student, I am the product of an excellent public education. I, too, feel a sense of urgency and obligation to our children, but I have an abiding faith in our schools and in our educators. The pragmatist in me knows that if you want to move people and systems to bring about academic excellence and lasting change, you begin by believing in those you lead. Many of the educational reforms today, even those inspired by the most dynamic, innovative, and capable leaders, are short-lived because these leaders fail to do the hard work necessary to include their school board and school community members in their efforts. A word of advice for these would-be reformers: people do not mind change; they mind *being* changed. Given the high rate of failed school reforms, it is high time for a fresh, new approach. An innovative kind of reform is needed—an "against the grain" reform that is focused on building relationships with the school board and school community to get long-lasting results that will improve the life outcomes of our nation's children.

I recognize that my philosophy is unlikely to be embraced by those school leaders who approach educational reform with guns blazing. They probably did not share my good fortune, having learned from educators who understood the complexity of systemic change in schools. My teachers and mentors believed in engaging people in the work and building the relationships to sustain these reforms. Sadly, many school reformers today are trained more like Special Operations Forces (SOF)—expert military units called in to deal with large-scale, high-risk, do-or-die situations. This approach to education is dangerous, and I place responsibility for the collateral damage in our schools squarely on the shoulders of those reformers who, eager to make a name for themselves, come armed with their tactical maneuvers and quick fixes. These school reformers have made a mess of education with disastrous consequences for our children, and it is time for this to stop.

It is true that where I stand on the issue of school reform is a unique if not radical departure from current educational trends, and my critics will say that this soft approach to education will not get our students very far. What I can tell you unequivocally is that the relationship-building strategies in this book work, people believe in them, and they get results. One of my former school board members put it this way: "We were dying for dignity, and the work we did together kept us in check and gave us the strength to be brave when we had really tough decisions to make in the best interests of children." By implementing the ideas outlined in the chapters that follow, I strengthened my relationships with the school board, they improved their relationships with one another, the educators who work in my school system have a greater sense of self-efficacy and job satisfaction, and all of this has positively impacted our students. As a result of our relationship-building work together, we are seeing happier, healthier children who are achieving more academically, socially, and emotionally than we ever thought possible.

We take pride in how well our students perform in Taunton. Our student achievement scores are competitive with those of our urban counterparts, more students are attending top-tier colleges and universities, we have the highest graduation rates and lowest dropout rates that we have seen in almost a decade, and we have been recognized for closing achievement gaps at a rate that is two to three times faster than that of the state.[14] This achievement becomes even more compelling when you consider that the number of students living in socioeconomically disadvantaged homes has nearly doubled in seven years (free and reduced lunch status has increased from 35% in 2006 to 57% projected for 2015), and we have some of the lowest per pupil expenditures in the state. The headline of a recent article in our local newspaper, "Despite Tight Budget, Taunton Schools Are Showing Results,"[15] is apropos given Taunton's dubious distinction of consistently ranking in the bottom 10–15 percent for per pupil expenditures in Massachusetts and receiving one of the lowest per pupil rates of any urban school system in the Commonwealth for six years in a row.[16] Despite these socioeconomic struggles, we are committed to building stronger relationships among the superintendent, school board, and school community, and as a result, our students continue to achieve more.

Building effective relationships with a school board is anything but easy; it is hard work that requires a deep commitment from the superintendent, who in many ways acts as a lead teacher. As a school leader, you must recognize the individual and collective needs of school board members, providing opportunities for them to learn and grow together. You must be willing to accept differences in how they learn, what they believe, and what they know and can do. You must be open to the ideas of your school board members and be willing to learn and grow yourself. This book underscores the belief that, even under the most difficult circumstances, with hard work and determination school leaders can collaborate with their school boards to build high-functioning, productive teams and create a culture of success.

If publications that promise quick fixes and magical thinking are your thing, this book is not for you. Your work as superintendent can be daunting, and building relationships with your school board is hard work, but it is hard work worth doing. For a superintendent, like an excellent classroom teacher, there are no easy answers, and as Heiftetz says, "[I]nstead of looking for saviors, we should be calling for leadership that will challenge us to face problems for which there are no simple, painless solutions—problems that require us to learn new ways."[17] If you want to build and sustain an unprecedented level of success, you must do so by slogging through with a slow, steady, and relentless rhythm and an unwavering focus on building effective superintendent–school board relationships to improve learning outcomes for all students.

It is my hope that this book will usher in a new way of thinking about educational reform and the importance of relationship building in this work. The chapters that follow provide you with a roadmap for building effective relationships with your school board. The strategies offered will help you and your school board build a productive team and develop a mutual respect for the work that you do. I recognize that the job of the superintendent is one of the most challenging and demanding today, and I share these ideas with you knowing that it will not be easy, but building effective school board relationships is some of the most important work you will do as a school leader. It is my hope that when you encounter those inevitable obstacles in your leadership that threaten to derail your mission, the relationship-building techniques in this book will prove useful to you and empower you to make a difference for the children you serve.

CHAPTER ONE

Prioritizing Relationships for Sustainable Reform

Despite length of tenure, one thing is certain, for good or bad, the system will survive the superintendent.[1]

—J. W. GARDNER

WHAT IMAGES COME TO MIND when you hear the words *educational reformer*? Do you think about a heavy-handed, no-nonsense, turnaround agent who goes into a district to fire its teachers, restructure the schools, and institute policy changes? Maybe for you the words evoke an image of a pro-union educational reformer staunchly opposed to testing and determined to stop corporate greed, corruption, and the privatization of public education. Education reformers on both ends of the spectrum draw clear lines of distinction about what they do and do not support. Some school reformers champion charter schools, demonstrate an overreliance on objective measures, and regard unions as adversaries. Others champion public schools and unions, decry academic testing, and rail against the for-profit corporate educational agenda. While these reformers do not seem to agree on much, those on both sides of the argument do have one thing in common: they know our schools must change in order to improve the life outcomes of all children, especially those who are poor and of color, yet many lack the relationship-building skills necessary to produce results that are lasting.

Educational reform need not be at the expense of relationships. Superintendents do not have to choose between bold and courageous leadership and developing solid, positive relationships with their school boards. It is quite possible to have both. School leaders just need determination and perseverance to simultaneously address reforms and relationships. Those who know how to build successful relationships with their school board may be better equipped to effectively address substantive challenges that matter most to our children today, like issues of social justice, educational equity, and closing achievement and opportunity gaps. No matter how capable the superintendent is in terms of the technical knowledge and skills required to do the job, lasting educational reform cannot happen without the backing and strong support of the school board.

Given the number of failed educational initiatives and the inability of reformers to effect wholesale turnaround in many school districts,[2] there is an obvious need for a new approach to educational reform. Superintendents who seek seismic shifts in education demonstrate, as Galbraith says, a "willingness to confront unequivocally the major anxiety of their people in their time,"[3] and they are right to have the same sense of urgency as contemporary educational reformers. Hard-charging, modern-day change agents like former superintendents Alan Bersin (San Diego) and Michelle Rhee (Washington D.C.), or Cami Anderson (New Jersey), the current (as of this writing) superintendent of Newark, are certainly not wrong to be passionate about the need for change in public schools, nor is it wrong that they are unwilling to spend the next decade tinkering around with our children's education—something they all suggested when responding to community outrage about their educational reforms.

While a sense of urgency is vital, here is what some school reformers forget: they forget that *sustainability* is a characteristic of substantive leadership, and the degree of a superintendent's effectiveness can (and should) be measured by what happens after she is gone. If you want the changes that matter most to your students to take root in the system, outlasting your tenure, a new school of thought is needed—one that favors an approach to simultaneously build relationships amidst reforms. This new way of thinking requires school leaders to be bold, courageous, and respectful of the school board and school community to better serve all students.

ROCK STAR STATUS ONLY GETS YOU SO FAR

A story that keeps repeating itself in urban areas both large and small throughout the country is the tale of the school reformer eager to make a name for himself. This story illustrates why we need a different type of change agent: one who is more attentive to relationships. Along those lines, let me share with you a not-so-unique story about an urban school superintendent who was hired by a school board, given a multiyear contract valued at more than a million dollars, and hailed as a "rock star" among school leaders. By many accounts, the superintendent was dedicated, hard working, and eager to make a difference for his school community and students. In his self-evaluation, he counted among his achievements his close ties with the teachers' union, his strong advocacy for the school system, and evidence that the district continued to outperform many of its urban counterparts. The school board members publicly recognized the superintendent's positive leadership attributes, and they gave him high marks on his performance review, lauding his stamina and work ethic; his dedication to the district's strategic goals; and his willingness to engage parents, teachers, and business partners in the school community.

Unfortunately, the positive aspects of his evaluation were not enough to create a happy ending for the superintendent of this school system. Despite the high marks he was given, the governing body was dissatisfied with his performance on a standard that trumps all others: the superintendent's ability to get along with the school board. The board questioned the superintendent's professionalism, and they suggested that he was incapable of remaining impartial and objective. They faulted him for his inability to refrain from public criticism of the school board, and six out of eight members gave the superintendent an "unsatisfactory" rating on the performance standard that measures his ability to maintain a pleasant and effective relationship with them. Only three short years after making his triumphant entry into the school system, the school board denied the superintendent's request for a contract extension, they paid him to leave his post a year early, and the bereft school leader was left to wonder just how and why his tenure with the school system ended so abruptly.

Stories like this are far too prevalent in the United States, but it is seldom the case that the superintendent is replaced for failure to make academic progress. In this era of educational accountability and reform, new research is emerging to suggest that superintendents who get results are losing their jobs because they do not understand how to build effective superintendent–school board relationships. In a study conducted by the American Educational Research Association in 2012, researchers were interested in learning more about the factors that predicted a superintendent's exit; the study examined the departures of 215 superintendents in California. Researchers found that school board members' views on how well the school board functioned and whether the superintendent came from within the district were strong determinants of "non-retirement exits." They concluded that "school board members' subjective evaluations of the superintendent's performance predicted turnover, but district performance did not."[4]

John Deasy in Los Angeles Unified School District, Rudy Crew in Miami-Dade, and Arlene Ackerman in San Francisco are but a few more superintendents across the United States who have been plagued by such controversial relationships with their school boards; they lost their jobs shortly after their appointments due to a brief tenure marked by public outcry and controversy.[5] The good news for these school leaders and others like them is that supply and demand works in their favor: the critical shortage of superintendents in the United States allows them to find work easily in other communities, no matter how tumultuous their previous tenure.

Some of these superintendents who experience relational hardships with school board members learn from their mistakes and become more successful in their next post, whereas others continue to be plagued by the same relational challenges that they encountered in the past. School reformers like these often convince themselves that termination from a top post is the casualty of the crusader—an unfortunate outcome that goes along with the job. While superintendent and school board disharmony may inconvenience a superintendent by putting his job in jeopardy, the real tragedy here is that the discord is certain to negatively impact the school system and its children.

THE HIGH PRICE OF SUPERINTENDENT TURNOVER

How unfortunate it is that school districts that can most benefit from decreasing superintendent turnover encounter it most frequently. There are approximately seventeen thousand school systems in the nation, and the Council of Great City Schools represents sixty-five of the largest urban school systems among them. These districts "serve approximately 7.2 million of America's 48.7 million K–12 students (14 percent) and approximately one-third of the nation's low-income students, students of color, and English language learners."[6] Superintendents in these "great city schools" experience turnover more frequently while they struggle to confront the needs of the majority of the students in our nation with the greatest set of challenges.[7]

Although the average tenure of a school superintendent has substantially improved during the past two decades, by and large the length a superintendent remains in any given district is still relatively brief. Researchers examined the longevity of superintendents in 292 school districts for nearly two and a half decades and determined the average tenure of a school leader was six to seven years in a school system regardless of the size of the district and its geographic location.[8] The tenure for an urban superintendent of schools drops sharply to only four years on average.[9] The average tenure drops to just 3.64 years for urban superintendents in one of America's larger cities like Atlanta, Baltimore, and New York City. Although the average tenure for an urban superintendent of schools is rather short-lived, the trend appears to be moving in the right direction now, as this number has nearly doubled since 1999 when a superintendent was expected to last only 2.33 years on the job.[10]

Voluntary and Involuntary Turnover

Anderson and Grissolm identify two types of turnover—voluntary and involuntary—and present evidence to suggest that voluntary turnover is a function of the current labor market, whereas involuntary turnover can be attributed to challenging superintendent and school board relationships.[11] Voluntary turnover occurs when a superintendent or school leader chooses to seek another job for her own personal gain. Perhaps she is interested in a higher salary, a shorter commute, a school system with greater resources, or more power and prestige in a position. Superintendents who experience a higher rate of voluntary transfers may be recruited more often because they exhibit greater skill and competency and have developed a reputation for themselves.

Turnover in either form may be collateral damage that is expected in private industry, but school systems are not designed to sustain such a loss in leadership. In the business world, chief executive officers come and go, and businesses wither and bloom under new leadership. Corporate giants with their board of directors, their profit margins, and their bottom line seem structured to weather high turnover rates in leadership; however, school systems responsible for the life outcomes of their children may not be so robust when it comes to withstanding an ineffective school leader. Today, public educators are not producing a work force for the industrial revolution; their mission is to produce an educated citizenry of democratic learners capable of contributing to a global society. This all-encompassing mission requires stable and capable school leadership.

When superintendent turnover occurs, do superintendents leave on their own accord, or are they invited to leave? How does a superintendent's departure impact school reforms? What are the implications for a school community? It appears that the answers to these questions are as complex as the work of the superintendent itself. Several factors contribute to a superintendent's exit from a school system, and it has been determined that approximately 60 percent of superintendent turnover is voluntary, which by implication means that 40 percent do not leave their posts on their own.[12] It also turns out that a good number of these departures can be attributed to a tenuous relationship between superintendents and their school boards.

Anderson and Grissolm suggest that "the 'pull' of career advancement must be considered alongside the 'push' of difficulties in the current work environment as an important contributor to superintendent exit."[13] The inherent challenges in the work may lead to involuntary turnover, which occurs when a superintendent does not get to choose whether she will remain in the job. The superintendent is not renewed, is forced to resign, or is even fired. More often than not, an involuntary transfer is the result of poor superintendent and school board relations rather than a function of the school leader's inability to establish the conditions necessary to attain district goals or desired student achievement outcomes.

HOW TURNOVER AFFECTS SCHOOL SYSTEMS

A growing body of evidence suggests that whether voluntary or involuntary, superintendent turnover negatively impacts a school system. A superintendent who is confronted with involuntary turnover and asked to step down from her post pays an obvious price. She may be faced with the prospect of unemployment, her ties to the organization (to which she likely feels some sense of attachment or she would have left on her own accord) are severed, her compensation and benefits are ended, and her future employability status may be adversely affected. Although the implications of involuntary turnover may be less obvious for the staff and students, they also pay a price when a superintendent's tenure ends, either voluntarily or involuntarily, and it turns out that the price is not inconsequential.

A superintendent's work is complex, and the vast responsibilities that come with the job include oversight of finances, facilities, politics, curriculum, instruction, and a whole host of additional obligations. Because of the nature of the superintendent's responsibilities, which are both widespread and highly specialized, any break in service contributes to a period of organizational instability; this instability triggers a setback for the school system until a new leader is appointed and some sense of stability is restored.[14] Successful systemic school reform takes five or more years of a superintendent's focus, and if reforms are underway when the superintendent leaves, a greater negative impact can result.[15] To put it plainly, it could be the case that a failed reform is worse than no reform at all.

In addition to the managerial implications of superintendent turnover, school systems also face significant cultural implications. The loss of a superintendent may adversely affect staff morale and employee job satisfaction, and this may have a trickle-down effect on principal and teacher turnover and performance.[16] The public's perception is also shaped by the media, which perpetuate the myth that superintendents do not last long in any given job, thus predisposing reforms to failure and creating the public expectation that superintendents will exit soon after their arrival.[17]

THE PROBLEM WITH EDUCATIONAL REFORM TODAY

Relationship building is not a new concept in the literature on effective school leadership,[18] yet few if any works focus on precisely *how* a superintendent establishes these successful relationships with her school board. While the importance of building relationships as a superintendent is addressed in the literature, it is done only in a cursory way. School leaders are encouraged to "form bonds" with school community members, but few if any authors give specifics on the strategies that superintendents can use to fortify relationships with school board members. Instead, they are left to sort through these sophisticated challenges on their own, along with a myriad of other demanding and highly complex tasks. "How to" manuals to help superintendents build sound organizational systems, fiscally responsible budgets, and cohesive and comprehensive curricula exist. There are even a few authors who attempt to address how to build effective superintendent–school board relationships; however, these efforts generally result in a hodge-podge of relationship-building advice taken from various practitioners in the field. There has never been a comprehensive playbook for building effective relationships with school board members.

There is no debate that educational reform is desperately needed in this country, and superintendents will be better equipped to tackle the challenges with an all-inclusive approach to relationship building. In the three decades since the publication of *A Nation at Risk,*[19] results have been the focus for policy makers and the public, and accountability for student performance remains one of the foremost topics in educational policy today. This preoccupation with outcomes is understandable given the fifty-year achievement gap that still plagues our nation[20] and the continued decline in test scores on the National Assessment for Educational Progress (NAEP), placing the United States further behind its international counterparts.[21] With society's growing demands and a country consumed by results, what superintendent has time to worry about building relationships with anyone, let alone relationship building with her school board?

A national leadership crisis is emerging, and if we are serious about closing the achievement and opportunity gaps, superintendents today cannot continue to neglect relationships with key stakeholders, including their school board. With a fractured Congress and leaders of our nation unable to work together to resolve issues, it has become fashionable for school leaders and school boards to argue and fight, an unfortunate symptom of our times. Educational reformers may define themselves as change agents, anticharter advocates, data experts, pro-union activists, or turnaround specialists, but no matter what their philosophical bent, far too many poor superintendent evaluations, nonrenewals, votes of no confidence, short-lived reforms, and lackluster student achievement outcomes still exist, and the real losers here are children. This suggests that something is missing in the educational reform effort, and that something is superintendent and school board relationship building.

ANOTHER WAY: BUILDING RELATIONSHIPS, YIELDING RESULTS

Rock star reformers make changes with no long-term lasting effect, but relationship-building reformers make improvements that are enduring and live on well after they are gone. Earlier, I introduced you to a superintendent who was hailed as a rock star when he accepted the top job, only to be quickly shown the door when he was unable to maintain a relationship with his school board. The problem with rock stars is that they tend to take their loyal following and "insane talents" for granted, and they do not take the time necessary to cultivate relationships with their adoring fans. You might wonder how a superintendent finds the time to invest in relationship building when the leadership demands of superintendents today are growing at unprecedented rates.[22] Believe it or not, superintendents who are able to usher in the reforms and maintain close connections with their school boards do exist, and Andrés Alonso, former chief executive officer of the Baltimore Public Schools, happens to be one.

Stories of superintendent–school board disharmony are everywhere in the news these days, but it is nearly impossible to find examples of relationship-building reformers who radically alter their schools and improve the life outcomes for children, by connecting with their school board and school community. This unique leadership style leads to effective schools and successful children, and it is the point of this book, so I went looking for a superintendent who fits the mold. I wanted to showcase a leader who has taken on reforms so challenging that it would make another superintendent scratch her head and ask, "How on earth did you survive that?" This person also had to have a school board who—after experiencing these radical school reforms—would be able to say, "Our superintendent is the best thing that's ever happened to us."

While it is true that there are many outstanding school leaders across the nation, superintendents who have initiated radical reform and are considered relationship-building experts are hard to find. After doing an exhaustive search of school leaders across the country and repeatedly coming up short, I finally came across Andres Alonso and his story. As fate would have it, Alonso had just taken a job nearby as a Professor of Practice at the Harvard Graduate School of Education, so I contacted him to see whether he would be willing to meet with me, and to my delight, he said yes. I met him at his office in Cambridge and found him to be insightful, intuitive, and well versed in school reform—and everything education. It was clear to me in a matter of minutes that Andres Alonso was exactly the relationship-building reformer for whom I had been searching.

Learning more about what moves a person and his life experiences can illuminate the development of the qualities and characteristics that make a superintendent successful, and so I begin with the story of Andres Alonso's early years, which shaped the school leader he is today. In 1969, a few years after the Bay of Pigs Invasion, Alonso and his family emigrated from Cuba to the United States. Both he and his father worked in labor camps, and he was held back in the seventh grade after arriving in the United States because he was unable to speak

English. With the help of excellent teachers who believed in him, Alonso overcame the odds and later was accepted to Columbia University; he then went on to earn advanced degrees including a juris doctorate and a PhD from Harvard University.[23]

After a brief stint on Wall Street, Alonso realized he was unhappy in his job as a lawyer and discovered his calling was education. He quit his impressive corporate job and spent the next twelve years employed as a teacher of students with special needs in New York, where he became so invested in his work that he adopted and raised one of his at-risk students. Alonso had never been an administrator, but his deep passion for education was self-evident, and Chancellor Joel Klein recognized his potential, appointing him Deputy Chancellor for Teaching and Learning in the New York City School system.[24]

Alonso's responsibilities included oversight of the entire New York City educational system with more than one million students in over one thousand eight hundred schools,[25] but unlike other superintendents who must answer to a school board, he answered only to two individuals: the governor and the chancellor. Aside from a brief superintendent internship in Springfield, Massachusetts, Alonso had no practical experience or first-hand knowledge of working with a school board, but he was savvy enough to know that "getting to Baltimore was all about the school board" and he understood that "everything in Baltimore was political."[26] Alonso's life experiences helped him develop a sense of self-reliance that prepared him well for the challenges inherent in being a chief executive officer in a culturally diverse urban school system.

Alonso began his tenure in the Baltimore Public Schools by working to align his vision with the school board's and ensuring they had a commitment to transform. He is a rare leader with a knack for figuring out what problems to solve and how to tackle the toughest of school reforms. He knows instinctively the gains that can be made when a superintendent believes in school reform and adequately invests in building relationships with members of the school board and school community. During his five years in Baltimore, Alonso was able to accomplish more than most superintendents do in their entire career. He developed close ties with individual school board members, as well as the entire governing body, and he worked with his school board to establish a collective vision.

Alonso's relationship-building efforts helped him create a productive team and successfully institute sweeping educational reforms. He was able to significantly reduce central administration, establish a weighted funding model, reduce the dropout rate by 56 percent, obtain the best-ever graduation rates, stop the charter school mass exodus and its 2.5 percent annual decrease in enrollment (and all the financial challenges that went along with it), and close twenty-six underperforming schools.[27] And what's more, he lived to tell about it.

Perhaps the most impressive thing about Andres Alonso is that when he left his Baltimore post as the schools' chief to care for an ailing family member out of state, his school community was sorry to see him go. Unlike the rock star reformer whose school board promptly showed him the door, this relational reformer's school board and school community wanted him to stay on as their leader. Realizing his departure was imminent, and they could not convince him to stay, they held recognitions in his honor, the media wrote flattering articles about Alonso's transformation of the school system, and Neil E. Duke, Chair of the Baltimore City Board of School Commissioners, had this to say about him: "Under Dr. Alonso we have laid a foundation for sustained improvement, and today we are a much better school system thanks to his forceful leadership and extraordinary commitment to kids."[28]

EFFECTIVE SCHOOL GOVERNANCE

The practice may not be prevalent just yet, but as we have seen, it is entirely possible for superintendents to engage in extremely challenging reforms and still maintain close superintendent–school board connections in the process. What school leaders should ask is how do they achieve this result? What are the conditions of renewal and effective school governance that must exist to create high performing schools? A case study of several districts demonstrates that student learning increases when there is a districtwide focus on improvement, a clear definition of success, a system for monitoring progress, intentional policy development, and the implementation of a leadership continuum.[29] School systems with effective collaborative governance address challenges together, create innovative programs that enhance teaching and learning, produce high achievers, receive recognition and rewards, and cultivate a positive school culture in which students and staff members succeed.

Effective school governance may be harder to achieve now than it has been in the past because there has been no time in the history of public education that the work of superintendents (and school boards) has been as complex as it is today. Resources are scarce, funds are drying up, reformers are clamoring for change, the debates between public, private, and charter schools rage on, and superintendents find themselves inundated and struggling to keep up with expectations that run the gamut. They must hold high standards for teaching and learning, maintain high test scores, be masters of communication and public relations, possess exceptional fiscal management skills, and gain widespread support from the school community.[30] Efforts to increase student achievement and outcomes for all students have created tensions that are at a fever pitch, and as the Iowa Association of School Boards has noted, "the field has been tilted toward student achievement with pressure and accountability such as we have not seen before in the history of the nation."[31]

Effective school governance, then, must be a balance between relationship building and results. Defining this balance is difficult because a thriving school culture involves intangibles—a synergy between and among the superintendent, school board, and members of the school community. Exploring the characteristics of high performing superintendents and schools boards gives us insight into what it takes to produce high performing schools and school systems. Several years ago, a study was commissioned by the Iowa Association of School Boards to learn more about the ways in which superintendent–school board behaviors impacted student achievement.[32] Not much had been written on the topic at that point, and not much has been written on it since. This study, which measured the performance of several school systems, determined that the superintendent and school board behaviors played a role in student achievement, and certain conditions were present in "moving" and "stuck" (high and low performing) school districts.[33]

Conditions for School Renewal

The findings in the Iowa Lighthouse Inquiry revealed that seven conditions are present in high performing school districts: (1) an emphasis on building a human organizational system; (2) a perspective on how education gets better (i.e., how to make initiatives and support them); (3) a sense of how to create support around personnel as they carry out their roles; (4) a sense of how to build a human resources/staff development component to advance the knowledge and skills of personnel; (5) a sense of how to support school sites in the renewal process; (6) a sense of how to generate lay community involvement; and (7) a sense of integrative leadership (i.e., how to develop direction and focus from a realistic perspective), and the nature of strong but sensitive leadership. Further contemplated in the study were the behaviors of superintendents and school boards in both high and low performing school districts with respect to these seven conditions for school renewal.

Behaviors of Superintendents and School Boards in Low Performing Districts

In the low performing districts in the Iowa Lighthouse Inquiry, little evidence of a learning community existed, and an ambiguous relationship was present between the board, central administration, and staff. Superintendents and board members were highly responsive to mandates, and there was a lack of understanding about how to get certain initiatives off the ground. Superintendents and board members did not know how to show support for staff, and they frequently made disparaging remarks about the staff. They led in an "accountability mode," viewing personnel as something to be managed. There was no sense of how to support the staff in the change process, and there was an inadequate understanding of how to effectively engage the lay community in their efforts. Worse yet, the school board possessed a shared belief that it was *not* possible to increase community engagement. With a transactional view of leadership, the superintendents and school boards in these low performing districts considered themselves authority figures who gave themselves permission to lead with a "because I said so" mentality.

Behaviors of Superintendents and School Boards in High Performing Districts

In the high performing school districts in the Iowa study, the story was fortunately quite different. The superintendents and school boards in these districts had evolved into learning communities, sharing information freely and involving many others in decision making. There was evidence of growing relationships between the administration, the school board, and the building staff. Superintendents and board members had an understanding of how to sustain and maintain improvements. They had positive attitudes about personnel, and they were focused on helping all staff succeed. Staff development was valued and viewed as critical to the success of a reform. Superintendents and school boards were favorable to site-based initiatives, possessing an in-depth understanding of the work that was going on in individual schools. They felt strongly about the need to include the lay community in school reforms, and the superintendents and school boards believed in vertical/horizontal integration and increasing connections throughout the district.

A CALL FOR POSITIVE AND PRODUCTIVE RELATIONSHIPS

Relationships play a powerful role in successful reform, but a discernable difference exists between superintendent–school board relationships that are positive and superintendent–school board relationships that are both positive and productive. For the relationship to be positive and productive, the two parties must possess a sense of optimism and forge strong bonds to effect changes that are hard won. Positive and productive relationships happen when school leaders initiate bold educational reforms to meet the needs of all students, and they give equal time and attention to strengthening the relationships with their school board and school community. Unlike top-down leadership, unilateral decision making, and a "my way or the highway" attitude, effective superintendents and school boards understand the complicated nature of solving problems in "the age of complex accountability systems and changing student demographic trends."[34] These skilled superintendents know how to establish effective relationships with the school board and school community to transform their schools and get results.

We know that student achievement can improve when superintendents and school boards develop effective relationships, yet current approaches to school reform do not necessarily reflect this understanding. Interestingly, corporate giants are just starting to realize that a company is unlikely to flourish if its focus is strictly on the bottom line. Rosabeth Moss Kanter, a researcher from the Harvard Business School, conducted research on a dozen global business giants, including some high-profile companies like IBM, Procter & Gamble, and Cisco, to learn more about their organization's transformation. After conducting more than three hundred fifty interviews on five continents, Kanter and her colleagues concluded that "we are witnessing the dawn of a new model of corporate power." The findings suggest that businesses are now changing their approach from one that focuses on outcomes and top-down decrees to one that engages stakeholders in building relationships through a coordinated series of actions and alignment, shared values, and processes in common.[35] If big business is starting to figure out that transformations depend on positive and productive relationships in their companies, why is it not so obvious to those looking for ways to improve education?

It has been said before that educators are not in the business of making widgets; we are in the people business. Therefore, we should be able to recognize the importance of relationships to create success in our schools. Unfortunately, today's school reform movement still attempts to improve education by replicating mass production, assembly-line, Weberian business models characterized by hierarchies, bureaucracy, standard operating procedures, and other outdated strategies. Data analysis, project management, and the tracking of student achievement outcomes are but a few ways that education takes its lead from its counterparts in business. When new research arises, the field of education is notorious for lagging behind in terms of its understanding, and our profession is infamous for its inability to adapt and incorporate these new ideas into our current structures and systems. It is my hope that we will not have to wait another decade for our profession to realize what corporations have already begun to understand: the traditional approach to organizational transformation is not enough, and the key to school reform and student success is relationship building.

CHAPTER TWO

Laying the Foundation I: Pre-entry, Entry-plus, and Re-entry

The beginning is always today.
—*Mary Shelley*

THERE IS SOMETHING freeing about a fresh start. Do you remember your first day of school, or how you felt at the beginning of a brand new semester in college, at the onset of a new season, or the start of a new year? New beginnings instill hope and help you see what is possible. A new start gives you a chance to reflect on your previous accomplishments and change what needs to be improved. New beginnings also represent a powerful opportunity for superintendents to establish positive, productive relationships with their school community that set the right tone for the future.

Solid relationships are built on strong foundations, and there are important building blocks that school leaders can use to fortify superintendent–school board bonds. I designed three relationship-building strategies that I call *pre-entry, entry-plus,* and *re-entry* as a way to strengthen superintendent–school board connections in various stages of the relationship. Pre-entry is a useful frontloading strategy that you, as superintendent, can employ before you are even offered a job; the

PRE-ENTRY: A relationship-building strategy school leaders can use before they begin a new job to gauge a school board's position on reforms and create alignment.

PRE-ENTRY STEPS

1. Establish your priorities. Talk to people in the know, and read newspapers, blogs, and other social media to see whether you can determine the greatest school community challenges.
2. Turn the tables. Identify a list of the top three to five challenges and what is needed to address them. Ask school board members to identify the school community issues they feel are most in need of resolution, and explore their ideas for how best to solve these problems.
3. Test the waters. Reflect on the challenges you have identified on your own and with the school board, and create a list of the most pressing problems that you wish to address. Share your list of challenges with the school board, and ask them if you are on the right track. Ask for their ideas for how best to resolve these issues.

strategy helps you build early alignment with your school board around priorities and approaches to the work. The second strategy that I call entry-plus is similar to the entry plan process that many leaders have come to know, but what makes this approach different is its greater emphasis on complex problem solving and relationship building. Entry-plus helps you learn about an organization and its people and get a jump start on educational reforms, enabling you to build stronger bonds with your school board. The third strategy, I call re-entry, is a process that practicing and veteran superintendents can employ to correct deep misunderstandings; this approach allows you to start anew, re-establishing and strengthening your commitment to building better superintendent–school board relations. These three relationship-building strategies signal to a school board that you are a different kind of leader, one who will take on reforms to improve student success *and* make relationship building your top priority.

PRE-ENTRY: A WAY TO BEGIN BEFORE YOU BEGIN

If you are an aspiring school leader seeking relationship-building advice from an experienced superintendent, you might hear that it is a good idea to spend some time familiarizing yourself with school board members soon after you are hired. Practicing superintendents may suggest that you talk with your school board chair and plan a "getting to know you" dinner or a casual get-together with school board members and their partners. Some of the more seasoned superintendents might even advise you to create a formal entry plan soon after you are hired to help acquaint you with your school board and school community. Most likely, you will not hear advice on starting the work on reforms and relationships *before* you are officially appointed to the position, but in my mind, putting problem solving and relationship building on hold until after you start the job is a missed opportunity.

Prior to my appointment as superintendent of an urban school system, I used pre-entry to test the waters with a school board who had not yet offered me the job. When I received a call from the consultant of a search firm to see whether I was interested in the superintendency, my thoughts were not focused on the contract or the financial terms; instead, I spent time thinking about developing the right conditions for success in the job. I had worked in the district for one year as a central office administrator before moving on to take a position in another district, so I had more insight into what was needed to transform the school system than most others—and also many questions. During my time in the district, I had learned there were great people in the system, but as a result of a series of circumstances, it appeared that the environment had grown even more caustic, and if the school system's negative press was any indication, it looked as though not much had changed.

One of my colleagues told me he had read about the school district online in the local newspaper, and he asked me why on earth I would ever want to return. I wanted to be in the job because the people in the city had their hearts in the right place, and I believed that with hard work I could help make the school system better for children who needed it most. I also knew the position was an enormous undertaking, so I got to work early.

Before I was offered the job, I took the opportunity to share with the search firm consultants, the school board chair, and a few school board members (as appropriate during the search process) my concerns about the inappropriate dynamics that occurred during televised board meetings and about the poor superintendent–school board relationship that existed. I was honest and straightforward, and I shared my colleague's (an outsider's) view of the school system. I also expressed my concern that a superintendency marked by great turmoil and controversy could be a career-ender for me, so there was a great deal riding on my success in the district. I asked many questions, and I took the liberty of getting school board members' thoughts and ideas about how to confront our challenges and create a winning team; slowly a picture of reform and relationship building began to emerge.

The pre-entry approach is a relationship-building strategy you can use to gauge a school board's position on reforms and create cohesion before you begin a new job. By its very nature, this is not a strategy intended for practicing or veteran school superintendents; however, the more seasoned school leaders reading this book may find the concept useful in the sense that it underscores the importance of focusing on relationship building early, often, and through all aspects of your leadership. If you are a new superintendent or a veteran superintendent who is new to a school system, you can use three important pre-entry steps that I designed to help you get a head start on reforms and relationships before you officially start the job: (1) establish your priorities; (2) turn the tables; and (3) test the waters.

Establish Your Priorities

In the preceding chapter, I introduced you to Andres Alonso. I can think of no school leader who does pre-entry better. Prior to expressing interest in Baltimore's top job, Alonso learned all that he could about the issues and challenges confronting the school system. He said he was "ready—more than ready—for the challenge" of being the chief executive officer of Baltimore Public Schools, and although he had the top job in his sights, he did not want it badly enough to compromise his values and beliefs. Alonso and his school board wanted to eliminate the dropout rate, get students in college, and help all English language learners succeed. The one thing he knew he needed from the start was a strong commitment from school board members to have the courage to do right by these students they hoped to serve. However, he also knew that this degree of change is often hard won, and he was perfectly willing to walk away from the opportunity to serve as CEO if he and his school board members were unable to reach agreement on how best to serve the students in the community.

Turn the Tables

Given their ambitions, Alonso wanted to be certain that the school board would be behind him as he made difficult changes, giving him the courage to act in the best interests of the students, so unlike a typical candidate interviewing for a job, he turned the tables on his interviewers. After participating in formal and informal interviews with the search firm and school board, he would go home, reflect, and, at their urging, call school board members with more follow-up questions. In Alonso's words, "lips were touching skin now," and he knew the importance of getting the right answers to questions before he accepted the job. Throughout their communications, he asked them questions about how ready they were for change, how committed they were to school reforms, such as closing underperforming schools and eliminating the dropout rates, and how they would react to the inevitable public outcry from such changes. He listened intently for patterns, themes, and trends and analyzed the school board members' responses to determine whether they were on the same page and deeply committed to students.

Test the Waters

Next, Alonso began to test the waters, which was the start of a pact with his school board to clarify expectations for how they would work together. When superintendents become finalists in a search process, it is sometimes the case that there is an opportunity to interact more directly with school board members, and Alonso took full advantage of this. Although his approach was not overt or obvious to board members, he started to make connections and build consensus around educational reform issues that would make a difference for the children in the Baltimore Public Schools. He wanted to know where school board members stood on the need to be united when a difficult vote was taken, how they would respond to community pressure when he announced the closure of a failing school in their neighborhood, and the type of support they needed from their leader in order to do this very difficult work. He then watched, listened, and learned to see how the school board would react to his questions and how quickly they were able to coalesce as a team. This pre-entry work enabled Alonso to develop consensus among school board members at the onset of his tenure; this, in turn, helped him shore up his relationships with the school board and make tremendous headway on significant school reforms early in the game. Eventually, he was offered the job and was satisfied enough about his ability to work collaboratively with the school board that he accepted the position.

Pre-entry is a way for you to foreshadow future reforms and clarify expectations for how you and the school board will work together. The approach to pre-entry is not overt for a reason; it can be off-putting to a school board if a superintendent who has not yet been offered a job comes armed with a survey or a list of questions for them to complete. Pre-entry is a relationship-building strategy that helps you work with your potential school board to set expectations in a natural, organic way. Most school boards appreciate the informal conversations about the important work ahead of them, and pre-entry is a good way for you to get an early start on building the kinds of relationships that help your students succeed.

ENTRY-PLUS FOR A JUMP START ON RELATIONSHIP BUILDING

During the last decade, the concept of entry planning has become as fashionable in educational leadership circles as it has become for a politician to report on his first one hundred days in office. According to Jentz and Murphy, the entry plan "is designed to slow things down in order to counter the external pressures and internal responses that inexorably lead to jump reflex problem solving" or rash decision making. The authors identify various types of learning that emerge during the entry-planning process "learning about your new place; learning about yourself; and collective learning about the organization as a whole."[1] This entry plan approach addresses piecemeal attempts to problem-solve rather than how to create systematic reforms that enable you to improve your superintendent–school board relationships. By contrast, entry-plus helps you reflect and learn about the needs of the organization, approaching reform systemically and taking action to strengthen superintendent–school board connections. If done well, the entry-plus process can be a catalyst for tackling significant school reforms, creating a productive superintendent–school board team as you work to transform your schools.

> ENTRY-PLUS: A process superintendents can use to reflect, learn about the needs of an organization, and take action on meaningful reforms, while strengthening superintendent–school board relations.
>
> ENTRY-PLUS STEPS
>
> 1. Communicate your intentions to the school board.
> 2. Design a plan.
>   - Identify school board members and other key stakeholders in the school community.
>   - Develop a unique set of questions to ask members of the school board and community.
>   - Create a timeline.
> 3. Publicize your plan.
> 4. Begin the data collection process.
> 5. "Cook," or synthesize, your notes. Identify patterns and themes in your data.
> 6. Prioritize and test your ideas.
> 7. Use your data to inform the norms, protocols, and strategic plan.
> 8. Communicate your findings.

Before I get into the specifics of entry-plus, it may be helpful to explore traditional entry plans in more detail. Entry plans were originally intended to help principals (not superintendents) get their start in a new position when they were unsure how to begin; the process was later adapted for superintendents and other school leaders. The concept of entry planning by school leaders originated with Jentz and Murphy, who recommend five steps in the process: (1) designing the entry plan; (2) seeking feedback; (3) getting the word out; (4) performing interviews and site visits; and (5) convening sense-making meetings.[2] The idea was for principals to develop a set of questions they could ask various members of their school community to help them be more reflective and demonstrate their ability to be good listeners. Jentz and Murphy characterized it as a "listening tour" of sorts, and the entry plan was designed with the names of interviewees and specific questions the principal intended to ask so that he could seek feedback from the school community on strengths, opportunities for growth, and his future plans. Once the school community weighed in on the leader's plan design, he would then start spreading the word about his entry plan. Next, he would conduct interviews and site visits to gather data and get to know the community better. Finally, he would

EXHIBIT 2.1 Superintendent's entry plan letter

SUPERINTENDENT'S ENTRY PLAN

Julie Hackett, Ed.D.

Dear Taunton School Community:

I am deeply honored that you have chosen me to be your new Superintendent of Schools, and it is a privilege to return to Taunton, a community about which I care deeply.

As I begin the process of acclimating myself to the Taunton Public Schools in my new role, I want to get to know members of our entire school community. To that end, I have developed this formal entry plan, which is an opportunity for me to learn from all of you. I am eager to hear your thoughts about our strengths and challenges, and your hopes and dreams for the future.

In the upcoming months, through a series of interviews with the Taunton School Committee, administrators, staff, students and others, I plan to get to know our school community better, as well as the work that needs to be done. I will conduct site visits at each of your schools, and gather information through document analyses, an on-line survey, interviews, and focus groups. I expect to share what I have learned from you and others through this process in a final community presentation in November.

This Entry Plan will assist me in developing a leadership plan that addresses our school system's most pressing needs; in addition, the information gleaned will inform our strategic plan. The Strategic Plan of the Taunton Public Schools will be our "blueprint for the future," representing our collective beliefs. It will clearly define our fundamental values, what we hope to do, and how we plan to achieve our goals.

Many thanks in advance for your support of me and the important work we will do together. As your superintendent, I look forward to honoring Taunton's past traditions and working with you to find new and exciting ways to give the very best to our children.

Sincerely,

Julie Hackett

Julie Hackett, Ed.D.

ENTRY PLAN TIMELINE

MAY

- School Committee Interviews
- Central Administrators' Interviews

JUNE

- Central Administrators' Interviews
- Principals' Interviews

JULY

- Community Members' Interviews
- On-line Community Survey

AUGUST

- Staff Interviews

SEPTEMBER

- School Site Visits
- School Community Focus Groups

OCTOBER

- School Site Visits
- School Community Focus Groups

NOVEMBER

- Community Presentation of Findings

"convene sense-making meetings," gathering constituents together to explain what he had heard during the interviews and to obtain their input.

The Jentz and Murphy entry-planning process is designed to slow down a school leader's tendency to engage in impetuous decision making and "change for the sake of change," and it remains a useful framework for school leaders. However, traditional entry plans do not address the practical ways in which you can use the process as a catalyst for change and a way to improve relationships with the school board and community. Entry-plus is designed to help you take action, address reforms, and build relationships with members of your school board and school community. I use familiar elements to those in the Jentz and Murphy model, such as plan design, community input, data collection, and communication of the findings, but the main focus of entry-plus is how you can initiate successful, systemic school reform and, at the same time, build stronger relationships with your school board members.

Entry-plus comprises eight important steps for school leaders: (1) communicate your intentions to the school board; (2) design a plan; (3) publicize your plan; (4) begin the data collection process; (5) "cook," or synthesize, your notes; (6) prioritize and test your ideas; (7) use your data; and (8) communicate your findings.

Step 1: Communicate Your Intentions to the Board

Begin by communicating your intentions to the school board to let them know that you are about to embark on an entry-plus process. I recommend writing a cover letter like the one in exhibit 2.1 to explain the various steps in the process that you will use, your timeline, and any other information that you think might be helpful. School board members may not necessarily have a clear understanding about what you are doing and why unless you tell them up front, so be sure to make your intentions explicit, using the information you glean to improve your schools and strengthen your relationship with the school board.

Step 2: Design a Plan

Getting started on the entry-plus plan involves three important actions: (1) identify school board members and other key stakeholders in the school community;

(2) develop a unique set of questions; and (3) create a timeline. When you make a list of stakeholders whom you would like to interview, start by thinking about the sphere of influence in your community: school board members, the mayor, city officials, students, staff, administration, business partners, union leaders, parent advisory groups, special interest groups, and others.

After you have made a general list, be sure to ask your school board members for advice about whom in your school community you should interview. This communication will reinforce for school board members that they are valued and respected members of the team. It will also be helpful to you because they will give you names of community members that you may never have considered, making your plan that much more thorough and thoughtful. Next, you can begin to tailor questions to each group of individuals to whom you will be speaking. What specific questions do you have for your school board? What do you need to know from union officials? What can you learn from central office and school administrators? What can you learn from teachers? Who should have your undivided attention, and who might you be able to meet with in a group?

Finally, develop a timeline for meeting with each person or focus group. Members of the school board and school community will appreciate the opportunity to have your undivided attention, so be sure to leave an additional window of time between interviews. Reflection has a funny way of bringing out the personal, internal struggles in people, so keep in mind that some interviewees may need a little extra time with you as they sort out their feelings. Finding the time to complete the entry-plus process can be one of the most challenging aspects of this relationship-building strategy. In one school system, I was able to negotiate an extra ten days ahead of my scheduled start date to do entry-plus, and this additional time gave me an opportunity to meet with over fifty people and learn more about the school system than I could have hoped. Using this approach was a great way for me to learn about the organization and its people, laying the foundation for our work together.

Whenever possible, I highly recommend individual, face-to-face meetings because it is difficult to build relationships and be a successful school leader without this personal touch. My school leadership motto is "people before paper," a mantra I share often with my administrative team. The more people feel they know you, the better off you will be when it comes time for you to make difficult decisions essential to creating better opportunities for the students you serve. In some cases, you may want to establish a focus group rather than an individual interview. I primarily conducted individual interviews because I believe relationships are strengthened when you give a person your undivided attention, but on some occasions focus groups were more appropriate. One focus group was with the Special Education Parent Advisory Committee, as a result of scheduling constraints and the nature of their shared interests. The data generated from this meeting later became an important driver in our school reform effort to move toward a district model of inclusion.

Step 3: Publicize Your Plan

Let the school board and school community know about your entry-plus process. A good way to publicize your plan is at a televised school board meeting if that medium is available to you. If not, see whether you can schedule some time to talk about your entry-plus process on a local radio or television station. When you explain the process, share with your audience how important it is for good leaders to listen and reflect and how important it is to you that the community has a say in their schools. Educators know all too well that communities today are skeptical of public education and superintendents, especially in urban areas where the tenure of the schools' chief has historically been short-lived. The skeptics may be even more critical if you are new or "from away," and most will not expect you to take an interest in their history and community. Many will expect you to arrive with your new bag of tricks, turn their world upside down, and then abruptly depart. Imagine their surprise when they hear you talking about how you want to know more about their past, learn all that you can from them, and work together to make changes that are important to them and the children in their community.

Step 4: Begin the Data Collection Process

It is now time to start the data collection process and begin your interviews and conversations with the school board and school community. I happen to enjoy taking notes because it helps me focus and listen more intently; however, I recognize that note taking is not for everyone. Since the entry-plus process is about building relationships, I do not recommend bringing an administrative assistant in the room with you to take notes because having another person there will be distracting and your interviewees may be more guarded. If you find you need additional note-taking support, consider using a tape recorder and have someone transcribe the notes at a later date. If you choose this approach, be sure to ask all the interviewees for permission to record them and explain why you are doing so. Asking permission to record someone's voice is not only courteous but is also the law in some states, such as Massachusetts. If you do take your own notes, be mindful of the need to monitor your note taking for bias. You may unintentionally avoid writing down certain aspects of your interviews because the topic is not interesting to you, or it is one of those contentious issues that you would rather avoid altogether. I try to write down everything I hear initially and reflect on the information later.

Step 5: "Cook," or Synthesize, Your Notes

When I was in graduate school studying qualitative and quantitative analysis, I learned how to "cook," or synthesize, my notes. Essentially, this means that you examine the transcripts of your interviews and site visits, look for emerging patterns and themes, and begin to code your notes. When I do entry-plus, I use highlighters to identify patterns and themes. For example, when I met with the school board, central administrators, principals, union, and Special Education Parent Advisory Committee, everyone spoke about the need to get special education spending under control. I went back and "cooked" my notes from all the various groups, highlighting in yellow any reference to financial issues in special education. I then pulled these data points into the "special education financial issues" category as supporting evidence that there was a widespread community desire to address this challenge.

Step 6: Prioritize and Test Your Ideas

As patterns and themes begin to emerge, you will develop a sense for the community's understanding of what matters most. Listening to these themes is important, but so is keeping in mind that you are the superintendent who is paid to have a vision and lead. Your intentions must be carefully balanced with the needs of the community, but as you develop a list of priorities, many of which should revolve around the desires of your school board and school community, be sure also to rely on your own experience and insight. For instance, the top priorities for the school board and school community might be getting a handle on special education expenditures by developing in-house programs, improving school safety and adding more staff during recess, or purchasing a new elementary reading program that aligns with the new state standards. Your top priority, on the other hand, might be to deal with the alarming number of students dropping out of school. It can be hard to publicly examine the school system's flaws and weaknesses, so this may not be a topic of discussion that is of interest to many. However, it should be included in your list of priorities because you know that ensuring that all students earn a high school diploma is a priority.

Your job as a school leader is to be a voice and advocate for all students, ensuring opportunities for those who are disadvantaged, as well as those who are from more privileged backgrounds—even if this creates dissension among school board and school community members. Superintendents are teachers in their school system who must help others develop new understandings and insights and a collective belief that can lead to a better tomorrow for the children they serve. Although such data may not be explicitly stated in your entry-plus interviews, there may be data in your transcripts that will help you support the ideas you have in mind. For instance, your interviewees are likely to talk about issues that relate to dropout prevention, such as student apathy or teacher performance; these important data points will present opportunities for you to link school community feedback from interviews to your own dropout-related concerns, demonstrating community awareness of the issue.

Step 7: Use Your Data

By now, you should have a treasure trove of data from your many interviews with the diverse constituency in your school system. I try to find as many ways as possible to use data I have collected for two reasons: (1) data collection is hard work for you and the person you are asking to provide it; and (2) data can have multiple uses and interpretations. Educators are busy, and not everything done in schools must have its own survey, interview, focus group, or poll. So get ready to use the answers to your interview questions and site visit observations as a useful source of data when you begin to co-construct the superintendent–school board norms and beliefs, and then plan to use the data again as you develop or revise the district's strategic plan.

Step 8: Communicate Your Findings

Your constituents will be curious about what you learned during your entry-plus process, so it is important to report back to the school board and school community to share your findings. If relationship building is the goal (and I hope that it is), a face-to-face conversation with the school board about your entry-plus plan is important because the discussion around what you learned presents another opportunity to coalesce as a team. You can also let the school community know about your findings by hosting a community forum; presenting on a local radio or television program (including a televised school board meeting); or by publishing your results in a newsletter, on the Web site, or through social media.

RE-ENTRY: YOUR SECOND CHANCE TO MAKE A BETTER FIRST IMPRESSION

We are all familiar with the adage "you never get a second chance to make a first impression." The fact is, school boards and people in general are usually more forgiving than you think—and if you use re-entry, you always get a second chance to make a better first impression. *Re-entry* is a powerful approach that practicing and veteran superintendents can use to signal a new beginning, transforming their lackluster school board relationships. Re-entry is a "mid-course correction" of sorts, as described in more detail in chapter 8. Odds are you will encounter an issue that may threaten to derail your relationship with the school board at some point in your superintendency because you are in the business of making difficult decisions. *Re-entry* is one strategy you can use with one or more members of your school board or the entire group to help prepare for that inevitability—and all it requires is a little honesty, bravery, and sincerity.

I once floated the idea of a policy change for honors placement at a school board meeting, which, much to my surprise, left some school board members extremely upset. I had taken the extra time to call every school board member in advance of the meeting to explain that the item on the agenda was meant to be the start of a conversation, reassuring board members that no changes were in the works. In my mind I was simply floating the idea and no decisions had been made; in some of their minds, I was changing a program that they had fought so hard to keep many years prior. Given their history with this particular issue, they believed my proposed changes might be a done deal. It was apparent to me that a serious rift was growing as a result of this misunderstanding, so I used the concept of re-entry to get a fresh start with my school board.

I reached out to each board member who was upset, first acknowledging that my delivery of the information could have been better, and then apologizing for my lack of understanding around the historical issues related to the problem. I listened to their feelings and concerns, I shared my own, and I then asked how we could get our relationship back on track. Anger and fear quickly gave way to forgiveness, and school board members apologized for overreacting. I reassured them that policy was the purview of the school board, and changes would be made only with the consent of the majority—and only after further study and consideration. Although using re-entry can be uncomfortable and awkward, leaders who use it display a certain confidence that school board members and others in the school system respect. A superintendent who is confident enough to speak up when something goes not quite the way she plans, admits that she could have done a better job with an issue, and accepts responsibility for her shortcomings is a superintendent who succeeds.

Relationship building needs to start early if you are a school leader who wants to create effective schools to help your students achieve more. Pre-entry is a strategy you can use to begin making connections and building consensus around challenges even before you have a job offer. Entry-plus is a process that you can use to demonstrate you are listening, show how much you care, and build a sense of shared purpose in a comprehensive, systematic way. This approach is enhanced when you communicate and develop a course of action by sharing with the school community what you hear, what you think, and how you plan to act as a result. When your relationship with the school board gets off track, and you need a fresh start, you can exercise resiliency with re-entry, a powerful strategy for practicing or veteran superintendents who are experiencing relational challenges. If done well, pre-entry, entry-plus, and re-entry can provide valuable relationship-building opportunities, giving you a chance to strengthen your bonds with the school board and reinforce your commitment to the school community.

CHAPTER THREE

Laying the Foundation II: Norms and Beliefs Protocols

Never believe that a few caring people can't change the world.
For indeed, that's all who ever have.
—MARGARET MEAD

A SUPERINTENDENT I KNOW works for a school board that has norms and beliefs protocols in place but refuses to honor them. His board members have been known to bring up inappropriate information during school board meetings, including sensitive material related to personnel matters. They make it known that they have no respect for the superintendent, which gives the school board license to commandeer decision-making authority whenever they see fit. During public input, they grandstand and demand that their superintendent answer the public's questions on the spot. Their meetings last until well after midnight, and the superintendent–school board relationships are so tenuous that not even outside interventions have led to improved collaboration. The superintendent has given up on school board members and takes every opportunity to get the job done without involving them. Is there any hope for a dysfunctional team like this?

NORMS AND BELIEFS PROTOCOL

A relationship-building protocol co-constructed by the superintendent and school board to memorialize shared beliefs, values, attitudes, and behaviors.

MATERIALS NEEDED

- Sample norms and beliefs protocols
- Entry-plus school board interview transcripts

TEN-STEP PROCESS

1. Collect sample norms and beliefs protocols.
2. Study your school board.
3. Consider board members' unique characteristics.
4. Identify what matters most.
5. Review your entry data.
6. Hold yourself accountable.
7. Categorize norms and beliefs.
8. Develop a draft and communicate your ideas.
9. Get consensus on the norms and beliefs.
10. Establish ongoing opportunities for reflection and revision.

The answer is yes, but make no mistake that doing so will require a Herculean effort by the superintendent and an unwavering commitment to improving superintendent–school board relationships. For those ready to take on the challenge, the norms and beliefs protocol is another important part of a superintendent's relationship-building repertoire, which can help strengthen all relationships, even those as challenging as the one just described. The norms and beliefs protocol is a blueprint that is co-constructed by the superintendent and school board to memorialize their shared beliefs, values, attitudes, and behaviors. The entry-plus process described in chapter 2 is geared toward the individual needs of school board members and can be used to inform the norms and beliefs protocol. Unlike entry-plus, norms and beliefs are focused on the collective needs and working conditions necessary for the superintendent–school board relationship to thrive.

Norms and beliefs protocols are somewhat a trend nowadays among superintendents and school boards, with more of those working in school governance seeing the benefit of having a set of written agreements or expectations. The norms and beliefs protocol that I am recommending to you in this chapter is different from others because the emphasis on relationship building is greater than the superintendent's management of the school board. Protocols designed to control school boards are often implemented by superintendents (and sometimes school board chairs) looking for ways to keep people in check or to neutralize negative behaviors—a questionable practice for any school leader who hopes to strengthen relationships with the school board. As you will see in appendix 3.1 at the end of this chapter, the norms and beliefs protocol is unique in that it spells out expectations not only for the school board but also for you as superintendent, which is a good way to earn your school board's trust and respect.

To give you a better understanding of what is meant by norms and beliefs, let me share how my school board and I adapted a fairly common norm that can be found in most protocols today and used it to improve our superintendent–school board relationship. Protocols often include a "no surprises" norm to discourage school board members from springing last-minute issues or votes on you with little or no warning during a board meeting. This is an important superintendent–school board norm because surprise tactics may violate transparency laws and unfairly disadvantage you when you could benefit from lead time to contemplate an issue, before being asked to publicly respond to an inquiry or decide on the merits of a concern with limited information or time for reflection.

The "no surprises" norm that is seen in most protocols typically applies only to school board members, but I know first-hand that superintendents can be just as guilty of springing surprises on their school boards. The norm that we developed reflects expectations for both superintendent and school board:

> The Superintendent and School Committee recognize the importance of proactive communication and agree that there will be no surprises. If the Superintendent and School Committee members have questions or concerns, they agree to notify one another in advance.

When we first established this norm several years ago, I was occasionally confronted by the school board for not holding up my end of the bargain. I knew our norms and beliefs were working when one school board member used them to remind me that our "no surprises" norm worked both ways. This board member talked about the need for the school board to be forewarned about issues cropping up in the newspaper. This was a reasonable request, but at the time I was dealing with an overzealous newspaper editor who printed negative stories about our schools almost daily—and with little or no warning—making it nearly impossible to get out ahead of the press.

Norms and beliefs helped me hold myself accountable in a way that I might not have if the expectation had gone unwritten. I was determined to hold up my end of the bargain, so I searched for ways to stay true to this norm and address the school board's concern. I strengthened my relationships with the local reporters who helped alert me to possible news stories that might be printed, and I learned to develop a better feel for the issues that had the potential of becoming negative press. This approach, in turn, helped me create better communication strategies, as detailed in chapter 8, so I could give school board members the heads-up they needed to circumvent surprises and strengthen our relationship.

As seen in the previous example, the norms and beliefs protocol is a useful tool because it makes superintendent–school board expectations explicit, and it addresses the challenges that typically arise between school leaders and their governing boards rather than leaving them to chance. Yet, in many ways, the consensus-building process that goes into its creation is more important than the protocol itself. As the protocol is developed, you and the school board must work together to identify issues that matter the most to you, but collaboration and consensus building take time and patience. You are a lead learner who can teach the school board by example how to identify desired outcomes and needs, how to provide a rationale for why a particular issue or norm matters, how to listen intently to the other side, and how to compromise. Whether you are a brand new superintendent or have been a superintendent for the past three decades, the success of your school system often depends on the behind-the-scenes work you do to position yourself well for the inevitable challenges encountered by every superintendent and school board.

HOW TO DEVELOP NORMS AND BELIEFS

Relationship-building strategies like the norms and beliefs protocol can be counterintuitive in that the longer they take to develop, the more likely they are to benefit the superintendent–school board relationship. Relationships are developed by giving freely of yourself and taking time to listen and learn from the people who matter most to you. To build stronger relationships, you should avoid the quick adoption of a protocol, giving yourself permission to slow down the process.

You can take several steps to create and customize a norms and beliefs protocol to strengthen your relationships with the school board. The process identified in this section is one that worked for my school board and me, and it includes ten steps: (1) collect sample norms and beliefs protocols; (2) study your school board; (3) consider board members' unique characteristics; (4) identify what matters most; (5) review your entry data; (6) hold yourself accountable; (7) categorize norms and beliefs; (8) develop a draft and communicate your ideas; (9) get consensus on the norms and beliefs; and (10) establish ongoing opportunities for reflection and revision.

Step 1: Collect Sample Norms and Beliefs Protocols

Many superintendents and school boards today use norms, beliefs, and protocols to guide them in their collective efforts, easily obtaining samples with a quick Google search. When I first initiated the development of a norms and beliefs protocol with my school board, I tracked down five or six examples from other school systems across the country. I highlighted ideas, phrases, and stylistic features that might help to inform our norms and beliefs. In one of the sample protocols I collected, the norms were grouped into categories, a structure that I found useful and later incorporated into our protocol (see step 7). I encourage you to work with your school board chair to collaboratively identify the norms and beliefs that may be most relevant, which can later be incorporated into a draft. Superintendents and school boards have been known to collect samples and engage in the wholesale adoption of the protocols developed by others, but this is a practice to avoid because the process of developing norms and beliefs is as important as the protocol itself. If your goal is to build relationships and unify your school board, you will want to do the hard work necessary to customize your norms and beliefs, ensuring the protocol is useful, relevant, and meaningful.

Step 2: Study Your School Board

The more information you can learn about individual school board members and the collective body, the more likely it is that your norms and beliefs protocol will help you neutralize potential issues and create high-functioning teams. If you are a superintendent who is new to a school system, the entry process outlined in chapter 2 gives you a head start on getting to know your school board better. If you are a practicing superintendent familiar with your school board, you may not need this step because you already have insight into what your school board values and how they want to work.

Before I was appointed superintendent, I watched school board meetings online, I scoured the minutes of meetings, I studied blogs and other social media to learn the perceptions of parents and the community, and I read more newspaper articles on school board issues than I can count. This research and document analysis enabled me to identify the group dynamics and potential school board strengths and opportunities for growth. For example, after watching footage of contentious school board meetings in which disgruntled parents demanded answers to problems and board members made motions for administrators to address those problems during the board meeting, I must admit that I was concerned.

At the time, superintendent–school board relations were fraught with tension, and the school board did the best it could under difficult circumstances. In their new school leader, they wanted a person who would be responsive and address the community's problems and concerns. As the newly appointed superintendent of schools, I took this responsibility seriously. I knew it would take some work to undo the ineffective approach to problem solving that had been created, leaving the community with the impression that the superintendent was not interested in hearing their concerns. By researching and studying the school board, I was able to identify this potential problem that may affect my relationship with the board. The school board and I talked about the issue prior to our first board meeting, and then we developed norms together, including a more suitable way to structure public input by referring issues to me with the expectation that I would update the school board on our progress toward a resolution.

Step 3: Consider Board Members' Unique Characteristics

Members of school boards are supposed to think about the best interests of the students they serve, and they do. But they are also human beings who will gravitate toward individual interests. If individual school board members feel their needs are not being addressed in the norms and beliefs, they may be reluctant to buy in to the process. An approach I used to help me focus on individual board members' needs during the development of our norms and beliefs protocol was to make a simple seating chart and think about one or two topics that came to mind for each member. I thought about what was important to Allison, what Mark wanted more than anything else, and what mattered most to Pat, and developed norms around their interests. For example, one school board member continued to express concern about how much time was wasted in school board meetings, so I made it a point to address this issue in our norms. When board members know the superintendent has taken time to consider their individual needs, they develop greater trust in the process and interest in the team-building work.

Step 4: Identify What Matters Most

At the onset, it can be difficult for a superintendent and school board to decide what should be addressed in the norms, and chances are you will refine your protocol during the reflection process outlined later in this chapter. In addition to the samples you collect, it is helpful to brainstorm your hopes and dreams for the superintendent–school board relationship. I began by considering what I heard during the entry-plus process and reflecting on the issues I heard from the school board and community, such as a need for greater inclusion, less isolation of students with differences in substantially separate settings, an urgent need to get our financial house in order, and possible school closures and consolidations to address inequities throughout the system. I then thought about how difficult it can be for superintendents and school boards to address problems like these, and we worked together to develop this norm to prepare us for the challenges ahead:

> The Superintendent will seek comprehensive solutions to problems and will create clear structures for decision making. In the spirit of continuous improvement, these structures may be revisited at any time.

Another helpful way to get at the issues that matter most is to reflect on the challenges that surface most frequently in school board entry interviews. As I reviewed my notes, I noticed that some school board members expressed dissatisfaction with the former administration's disregard for subcommittees, and several members seemed to feel a sense of distrust about the way information had been shared in the past. They felt the administration had intentionally left them out of important communications that were shared only with privileged members, thus making it difficult for all board members to respond to their constituents. I worked with the school board chair to better understand the concerns, and we added two norms to address both of these issues in our protocol:

> We acknowledge the historic importance of subcommittees, and the School Committee and Superintendent agree to utilize them to focus on a particular topic in-depth and to prepare for presentation, deliberation, and possible action by the full School Committee.
>
> School Committee members agree to refer important questions and concerns they receive from members of the school community to the Superintendent. The Superintendent will investigate and provide all Committee members with the information needed to respond to an issue.

After we added these norms, I made certain that in every situation all school board members got the same information at the same time as their colleagues. Now I am pleased to report that the equitable sharing of information no longer seems to be a concern for the school board. However, it is important to keep in mind that norms and beliefs do not resolve every issue quite that quickly, and several years later our efforts to address subcommittee concerns continue to be a work in progress.

Step 5: Review Your Entry Data

During the entry processes described in chapter 2, I embedded specific questions in the school board members' interviews that would later inform our norms and beliefs protocol. I knew that for the protocol to be effective, it had to belong to everyone. Embedding questions in the entry-plus process also enabled me to develop a draft protocol early in our work together before any negative habits or patterns of behavior were formed. During my individual school board interviews, I asked three questions of each school board member: (1) Can you tell me about a time when the school board worked well together? (2) Can you tell me about a time when you didn't work well together? (3) Can you identify some changes that we can make (either right away or down the road) that might improve the way we will work together?

Developing a draft protocol based on my own personal beliefs and values would have been fairly straightforward, but that would have made it mine—not ours. It was important for me to get the early input from the school board through the entry-plus process, which then allowed me to create a set of draft norms and beliefs to use as a starting point for developing a collective vision around the superintendent–school board working relationship. I was able to use the interviews as a way to gain insight into the school board members' personalities, philosophies, and worries, helping me to identify norms that also reflected their needs.

Step 6: Hold Yourself Accountable

When developing norms and beliefs, you also need to hold yourself accountable. Norms and beliefs are about your work *with* the school board, not your expectations *for* the school board, which is a point that some school leaders miss. For this reason, norms and beliefs protocols can be a sensitive topic for school board members, especially if they feel that you are imposing your own set of rules on them. You can counteract this issue by creating explicit norms to hold yourself accountable and address the concerns of school board members. The following norm was created during one of our retreats when school board members asked how they could influence the presentation topics at board meetings:

> The Superintendent will share an annual planning calendar with School Committee members. If a member wishes to add an item to a future agenda, he or she will make a request to the Superintendent or School Committee Chairperson. In turn, they will consult other members, as well as the annual planning calendar to gauge interest and alignment.

After much discussion, the school board expressed a desire to have greater opportunity for input into what was being discussed at school board meetings throughout the year. Together the school board chair and I had previously planned for this input, and we were still able to do so, but the added step of creating an annual planning calendar for school board review made the process more transparent and inclusive. This helped school board members see what presentation topics were being considered and afforded them an early opportunity to weigh in on the planning.

Step 7: Categorize Norms and Beliefs

Once you have identified possible norms and beliefs from the samples you collected, your entry data, and the list of ideas you brainstormed, certain trends should begin to emerge. You will notice that many norms and beliefs are related in one way or another, and I have found it helpful to cluster this information to make the protocol more accessible to school board members and easier to refine in the future. It is more challenging to make practical use of a list of fifteen norms and beliefs than it is to make use of superintendent–school board expectations that are clustered into three categories as seen in appendix 3.1: how we govern, how we communicate, and how we improve. Try grouping together your individual norms with similarities, and in so doing take into consideration your unique needs and the relationship that you and your school board are trying to achieve. Perhaps the norms you group together involve active listening, reflective practice, or innovation. If so, consider clustering the information into categories, such as how people listen, reflect, and innovate. Grouping norms and beliefs in this way makes it easier for you and the school board to remember, access, and improve on the protocol in the future.

Step 8: Develop a Draft and Communicate Your Ideas

It is now time to create a draft that you will communicate to your school board. Consider completing this step in collaboration with your school board chair if that approach appropriately aligns with the role of the chair in your district. I point out this issue because I have worked with school boards that operate under a hierarchical leadership model with the chairperson taking a stronger and more active leadership position. I have also worked with school boards that operate under a distributive model of leadership in which responsibility is shared equally among experienced school board members who have worked in the school system or served on the school board for decades.

If your chairperson plays a more active role in leadership, be sure to collaborate on the draft set of norms; otherwise, it is acceptable for you to develop the initial draft on your own. The draft should have a strong emphasis on how you used the information from the school board members' entry-plus interviews to shape the draft norms and beliefs, and you should make it apparent that collaboration and consensus are your goals, which means the board will have plenty of opportunity to discuss and make changes.

Finally, communicate the draft proposal at a workshop designed specifically for this purpose. I do not recommend adding this discussion into a regular school board agenda because the setting may influence how individuals approach these conversations. I have found it more effective to separate relationship-building efforts from the typical day-to-day business that is addressed in monthly and bimonthly meetings. In your presentation, you should give an overview of the process used to develop the draft, discuss how the data from school board interviews have been incorporated, and give a brief explanation of each norm.

Step 9: Get Consensus on the Norms and Beliefs

Achieving consensus is easier when you have taken the time to study your board (see step 2). This analysis helps you develop a sound understanding of what it will take to create the conditions for an optimal working relationship. The likelihood of gaining consensus increases when school board members see their likes, dislikes, hopes, and desires reflected in the draft. Certain norms generate a fair amount of consternation, and when the school board is grappling with a particular norm and its implications, I reassure board members and encourage them to worry less about the language and more about their willingness to commit to a certain aspect. I encourage them to speak up if they know they will not be able to commit to something and to share their reasons why. This approach helps members of the school board overcome the stumbling blocks and achieve breakthroughs in the discussion, which leads to consensus. We may all have different opinions about a particular norm, and when school board members are encouraged to share their feelings openly about a given norm or belief, it can lead to compromise, consensus, and new understandings about ourselves and one another.

Step 10: Establish Ongoing Opportunities for Reflection and Revision

Norms and beliefs create ongoing opportunities for discussion, particularly if you build this expectation into your protocol. As shown in appendix 3.1, two important norms that have been included expressly establish ongoing opportunities for reflection and revision:

> We recognize the importance of honoring our agreed-upon norms and beliefs, and we agree to take responsibility for reminding one another when we get off track.
>
> The Superintendent and the School Committee agree to set aside time on an annual basis for self-evaluation and to review our progress toward adhering to agreed-upon norms and beliefs.

School governance can be demanding, and even with the best intentions, you can easily overlook the ongoing work that is required to sustain the relationship-building practices developed through norms and beliefs. It is essential to set aside time to reflect and revise norms and beliefs on an annual basis because they are only as effective as the time you put into them. As you will see in appendices

3.2–3.6, you can structure opportunities for individual and group reflections in many ways. Three methods I have developed have been particularly useful; they include self- and group-assessment using the protocols we have agreed on, norms and beliefs pre-work, and "My Burning Issues" protocols.

It can be challenging for school board members to open up about how well they are conforming to the agreed-upon norms and beliefs. For this reason, you are encouraged to have board members begin with a group-assessment, such as the one shown in appendix 3.2, allowing them to share their thoughts about the school board's progress as a productive team. The results of the group-assessment can be tallied and averaged to help you begin to prioritize the norms and beliefs that need your attention. With an average rating of 2.2, the "How We Govern" category (see "subcommittee" norm number four) received the lowest rating for effectiveness, making it a potential area of focus for the superintendent and school board, as shown in appendix 3.3.

Once they become familiar with the group-assessment process, you can encourage school board members to participate in a self-assessment designed to help them reflect on their individual values, attitudes, and behaviors as a member of the team. These results can be shared privately with you, the chair, or with the entire school board if the board member is comfortable doing so. Keep in mind that this is a high-stakes activity because you are asking school board members to share their individual strengths and weaknesses; their willingness to do so will vary based on personalities and levels of trust. Compiling the results anonymously can help make this a less-threatening activity for school board members, and it can be helpful for you to model how to complete the self-assessment openly and honestly.

Another method I have used that helps elicit important information from school board members is to assign norms and beliefs pre-work (see appendix 3.4) asking school board members to review the protocol and provide their reflections about each norm and belief prior to the retreat. I usually ask school board members the questions, completing the written portion for them during a phone conference or an in-person meeting, and I then compile this information anonymously. This is time well spent because the information is rich and detailed, I typically have a better understanding of individual and group issues, and school board members feel better about getting their concerns out in the open in a nonthreatening way.

Finally, the "My Burning Issues" protocol (see the sample and blank form in appendices 3.5 and 3.6) is one of the most effective approaches I have used to deal with stubborn issues that need final resolution. This is a structured and timed approach to problem solving in which a school board member identifies a singular issue related to the norms and beliefs, explains why it bothers him, considers what his colleagues would say about this, identifies possible solutions, and shares this with his colleagues, who are encouraged to listen and ask clarifying questions. We have been able to make considerable headway on stubborn issues by using this protocol, and it has been one of the best tools in our repertoire as we have worked to build a productive team.

We typically set aside time at our retreats to reflect on our norms and beliefs. As discussed in more detail later in this book, the retreats are typically held off-site at various locations. Since we want our retreats to be productive, we always have an agenda, which means we must post the meetings to ensure that there is no violation of the transparency law known as the Open Meeting Law in the Commonwealth of Massachusetts. When we hold our norms and beliefs meetings in a school, the public and media are welcome to attend in accordance with our state's transparency laws, which can be awkward. This does not occur frequently, but when it does, I encourage board members to be as open and honest as possible, and I find that it gives those in attendance a greater appreciation for the complexity of our work and what goes into the development of high-functioning teams. We typically hold our norms and beliefs meetings off-site in the homes of school board members or at other venues. The discussion and debate during these get-togethers can present some highly sensitive issues that can be difficult to navigate, but in my experience each time we take on these challenges, we are rewarded with better working agreements and improved superintendent–school board relationships.

HOW TO NAVIGATE TRICKY ISSUES

If developing norms and beliefs that improve superintendent–school board relationships were easy, everyone would do it. This approach is more challenging than most because it is not just a protocol; it is ongoing work that requires your continued commitment. You can use this effort to fortify your relationship with the school board and unify your team. So how do you orient a new school board member to the team's norms and beliefs, helping that member feel a sense of ownership at the same time? And what can you do when a school board member thinks this pedantic approach to relationship building has no relevance to the key issues and is unworthy of his time and attention? And how should you react when the needs and desires of one school board member are in sharp contrast to those of others?

You may find yourself in precarious situations as you try to navigate the tricky issues that arise when establishing norms and beliefs, but there are ways you can counteract these challenges. Three of the most prevalent challenges that you will encounter as you and your team develop your norms and beliefs include (1) how to assimilate new school board members, (2) how to thwart "touchy-feely" thinking, and (3) what to do when norms and beliefs become personal.

How to Assimilate New School Board Members

The introduction of new school board members can inspire the team to try new approaches and work to be even better, but new school board members can also make the norms and beliefs work that much more challenging. I have found that just when our team begins to internalize a set of norms and beliefs, a new member enters the fold, impacting the group dynamics in much the same way that one new student changes the dynamics of a classroom. On the one hand, the norms and beliefs protocol can help introduce a new school board member to the working agreements that the team has established; on the other hand, it can leave the new school board member on the outside looking in as he has not yet had a chance to weigh in on these agreements—and he may outwardly reject some of the ideas in the protocol, which is certainly his right.

So what can you do when you are confronted with this challenge? One of the most effective ways to address it is to name the problem and acknowledge it up front. Our biannual retreats coincide with elections, so we generally hold a norms and beliefs meeting a month or so after a board member has been elected to ensure that the new member can weigh in early on the process. Chances are your school board members have put an enormous amount of effort into establishing their norms, so they may be a little sensitive to changing the way the group does business based on the wants and needs of one board member. When school board members say that a norm does not work for them, it helps when you encourage conversation that explores why that is so. For example, we had one of these discussions recently, and the school board was trying to establish a norm around subcommittee participation and seating. When a newer school board member finally pointed out that his objection to sitting in a particular location was due to the fact that he could not hear well, his colleagues had a different understanding of the issue.

How to Thwart "Touchy-Feely" Thinking

Let's face it, even the mention of something like norms and beliefs may seem hokey or unsophisticated to you and your school board members at first. You might be thinking right now that your school board members will laugh you out of the room if you introduce a "touchy-feely" concept like norms and beliefs—and you might be right. I remember when I first introduced the idea to my school board, and one member who was not particularly thrilled about the relationship-building work began referring to it as "norms and dorms," which was probably not a term of endearment. Whenever we experienced interpersonal conflicts or undue tension, another school board member would say, "It's probably time for one of those Kumbaya things again, isn't it?"

I withstood these comments by maintaining a good sense of humor and keeping my purpose in mind. As superintendent, I knew that building a stronger relationship with my school board was my top priority because the school community takes its cue from the superintendent and school board about how they are expected to interact with one another, which in turn affects the entire school community and our students. I know from experience that when members of a school community work together in collaborative ways, schools and school systems increase their effectiveness and students achieve more.

One way I have been able to put the feelings of the school board into perspective is to think back to my middle school years when my physical education teacher incorporated a unit on square dancing into our lessons. I was a fifth grade student attending Mattanawcook Junior High School at the time, and this new approach did not match what my friends and I knew about gym class: we were supposed to play rough-and-tumble sports like kickball, flag football, and floor hockey, and I was supposed to get even with Jimmy Davis for taking me out in dodge ball the day before! What teacher in his right mind would expect me to dance with Jimmy in a physical education class? This new approach was awkward and uncomfortable because it was completely different from anything else my classmates and I had ever done, and none of us knew how we were supposed to act or feel about it. So I did what any self-respecting human being does when she does not know what else to do: I scoffed, sighed, and repeatedly rolled my eyes to adequately convey my disgust to the gym teacher . . . and I made sure not to tell my secret—I actually kind of liked square dancing, and the truth was it didn't bother me one single bit.

For school board members, the norms and beliefs experience can be a lot like square dancing in a gym class. It is completely different from what they know about school boards and the work they are expected to do, so working on interpersonal issues can be a work in progress. I did not mind that this experience was a bit of a running joke, as long as we continued to do the relationship-building work necessary to set a good example for our school community and keep our focus on the students. As it turns out, in our norms and beliefs discussions, the school board members who made fun of the process ended up making some of the most insightful and significant contributions that have been beneficial to us all.

To date, we have engaged in more than ten norms and beliefs workshops, and it is now becoming second nature for us to collaborate and find ways to problem solve any and all relational challenges. At our last retreat, we identified the issues that were problematic for our team, and despite strong views about the right way to address these issues, board members did not take others' points of view personally. There was a natural give-and-take that had not previously existed, allowing us to more easily reach consensus. In contrast to our first norms and beliefs discussion more than five years ago, there is a level of sophistication and skill that did not previously exist. We now have to work together to address these challenges and strengthen our team, making schools better for our students.

What to Do When Norms and Beliefs Become Personal

Initially, the norms and beliefs work is quite challenging. When I think back to the effort my school board and I took to establish our current practices, I am grateful that the work gets easier over time. At a recent school board retreat, we reflected on our first workshop when we attempted to refine our norms and beliefs. We tried to talk about what was challenging, but the discussion was difficult because we were still new at the process, and individuals were not accustomed to openly discussing interpersonal conflict, so some took the concerns expressed by colleagues personally. As with any school board, people are different and have strong opinions on certain issues. This was clearly the case during one of our norms and beliefs sessions when one member expressed concern about another board member grand-standing for the camera during school board meetings; this comment set off the other board member, and he took the criticism quite personally.

Maneuvering around discussions like this can take some effort. I always begin the conversation with a review of what is working well, what I appreciate about my school board members, and what we have been able to accomplish together that will help our students. This technique helps keep the focus on the collective purpose of the school board, and it reminds school board members of all the good that they do together. In those awkward and tense moments like the one described earlier (and if you do this work correctly, you can expect some), it is helpful for you to neutralize the tension by reassuring others that it is better to address these issues truthfully and directly than allowing them to linger, creating embarrassment and more problems down the road. In moments like this, I acknowledge that the discussion is uncomfortable and tense, but it is absolutely necessary for us to function productively as a team. Humor can bring a sense of stability and equilibrium to a tense discussion, and I have found that when the timing is right, a joke or two about how the situation reminds me of one of my family feuds can help. School board members are usually quick to recognize that resolving the issues away from regular business meetings is also far better than letting these issues fester, while we are trying to conduct business at school board meetings.

Tensions can arise around all aspects of these conversations, including whether the norms and beliefs are being honored or if new ones are needed, and in my experience the superintendent can also counteract these issues by preparing for the discussion ahead of time. I make it a point to discuss ground rules and collaborative norms for the conversations, prior to any challenging discussion that I anticipate (see appendix 3.7), and when we encounter obstacles during the discussion, I gently remind school board members about the importance of following the ground rules and collaborative norms we set for ourselves. I also try to anticipate the issues that might come up based on my observations during board meetings or conversations with school board members, and I develop a well-thought-out agenda (see appendices 3.8 and 3.9) to help me structure the discussion in such a way that is a little less intimidating or threatening for school board members.

Norms and beliefs examine superintendent–school board attitudes and behaviors, which might make this one of the most challenging relationship-building strategies recommended in this book. School board members do not like to be managed any more than superintendents do, and school leaders sometimes make the mistake of using norms and beliefs protocols as a way to control or impose their own beliefs, values, attitudes, and behaviors—an approach that may cause feelings of resentment among the school board members, which is understandable. You must be willing to hold yourself accountable to the norms and beliefs if you want school board members to buy in to the process. When you and the school board work together to develop your own norms and beliefs, your relationships will be strengthened, and you will be better prepared to weather the obstacles that confront all of us in school leadership and governance today.

TAUNTON PUBLIC SCHOOLS—NORMS AND BELIEFS Updated March, 2014

How We Govern

1. We acknowledge that a School Committee meeting is a meeting of the School Committee that is held in public—not a public meeting, and we will make every effort to start and end meetings on time and ensure that they are effective and efficient.

2. School Committee members agree to thoughtfully seek and support solutions that will provide the greatest benefit to students. Once the School Committee has taken action, Committee members will support the official position of the School Committee.

3. It is the responsibility of the Superintendent to oversee the hiring, evaluation, and handling of personnel issues; it is the responsibility of the School Committee to evaluate the Superintendent's effectiveness in these matters.

4. We acknowledge the historic importance of subcommittees, and we agree to utilize them to focus on a specific topic in-depth and to prepare for presentation, deliberation, and possible action by the full School Committee. School Committee outreach is a way to show the community that we care. As appropriate, subcommittee members are encouraged to attend relevant school-based meetings from time to time.

5. If it is determined that a subcommittee could benefit from increased participation of School Committee members, it will be posted as a Committee of the Whole meeting followed by the name of the subcommittee. The chair of the given subcommittee will chair the Committee of the Whole meeting if the topic for discussion pertains only to his or her subcommittee.

6. School Committee members agree to recognize and respect that their authority exists when a quorum of the Committee meets and not as individual Committee members.

How We Communicate

1. It is our responsibility to set the tone for the entire school system, and we will make every effort to promote a positive image for our school system. The Superintendent will be visible in the community, and we will operate transparently and respectfully, maintain confidentiality, and respect the Open Meeting laws.

2. The Superintendent and the School Committee recognize the importance of proactive communication and agree that there will be no surprises. If School Committee members have questions or concerns, they agree to contact the Superintendent well in advance of a meeting.

3. We agree that discussion will be limited to the agenda, and items will not be added to the agenda unless it is determined by the Superintendent and the School Committee Chairperson that it would be detrimental to delay the issue until a subsequent meeting.

4. The Superintendent will share an annual planning calendar with School Committee members. If a member wishes to add an item to a future agenda, he or she should make a request to the

TAUNTON PUBLIC SCHOOLS—NORMS AND BELIEFS Updated March, 2014

Superintendent or the School Committee Chairperson. In turn, they will consult other members, as well as the annual planning calendar to gauge interest and alignment.

5. School Committee members agree to refer important questions and concerns they receive from members of the school community to the Superintendent. The Superintendent will investigate and provide all Committee members with the information needed to respond to an issue.

6. School Committee members will channel requests for information, reports and data through the Superintendent and the School Committee Chair rather than directly to staff. The Superintendent will ensure that each member has equal access to this information.

7. The Superintendent intends to seek comprehensive solutions to problems and will create clear structures for decision making. In the spirit of continuous improvement, these structures may be revisited at any time.

8. The Superintendent and School Committee recognize the importance of working collaboratively with City officials to improve our schools, and we will actively seek ways to enlist their support in our efforts.

How We Improve

1. School Committee members and the Superintendent recognize the importance of professional growth and development, and they agree to participate in experiences designed to further their knowledge and understanding and to advance the work of the Taunton Public Schools.

2. In addition, School Committee members will participate in formal training organized by the Superintendent and the School Committee Chairperson and conducted by organizations such as the Massachusetts Association of School Committees (MASC) and/or Massachusetts Association of School Superintendents (MASS).

3. All new School Committee members will participate in an orientation session, and if desired, a School Committee mentor will be assigned.

4. The Superintendent and the School Committee agree to set aside time on an annual basis for self-evaluation and to review our progress toward adhering to agreed-upon norms and beliefs.

5. We recognize the importance of honoring our agreed-upon norms and beliefs, and we agree to take responsibility for reminding one another when we get off track.

APPENDIX 3.2 TPS Norms and Beliefs Self- and Group-Assessment

TPS Norms and Beliefs Self- and Group-Assessment

Directions: Review and reflect upon the Norms and Beliefs under each category: (1) How We Govern; (2) How We Communicate; and (3) How We Improve. On a scale of 1 to 4 (1 being the lowest), rate your individual progress toward this indicator, as well as the progress of the group. If an indicator applies only to the Superintendent, it is not necessary to rate that indicator.

HOW WE GOVERN

INDICATORS	RATINGS				
1. We acknowledge that a School Committee meeting is a meeting of the School Committee that is held in public—not a public meeting, and we will make every effort to start and end meetings on time, and ensure that they are effective and efficient.	**INDIVIDUAL**	1	2	3	4
	GROUP	1	2	3	4
2. School Committee members agree to thoughtfully seek and support solutions that will provide the greatest benefit to students. Once the School Committee has taken action, Committee members will support the official position of the School Committee.	**INDIVIDUAL**	1	2	3	4
	GROUP	1	2	3	4
3. It is the responsibility of the Superintendent to oversee the hiring, evaluation, and handling of personnel issues; it is the responsibility of the School Committee to evaluate the Superintendent's effectiveness in these matters.	**INDIVIDUAL**	1	2	3	4
	GROUP	1	2	3	4
4. We acknowledge the historic importance of subcommittees, and we agree to utilize them to focus on a specific topic in-depth and to prepare for presentation, deliberation, and possible action by the full School Committee. School Committee outreach is a way to show the community that we care. As appropriate, subcommittee members are encouraged to attend relevant school-based meetings from time to time.	**INDIVIDUAL**	1	2	3	4
	GROUP	1	2	3	4
5. If it is determined that a subcommittee could benefit from increased participation of School Committee members, it will be posted as a Committee of the Whole meeting followed by the name of the subcommittee. The chair of the given subcommittee will chair the Committee of the Whole meeting if the topic for discussion pertains only to his or her subcommittee.	**INDIVIDUAL**	1	2	3	4
	GROUP	1	2	3	4

1

TPS Norms and Beliefs Self- and Group-Assessment

6. School Committee members agree to recognize and respect that their authority exists when a quorum of the Committee meets and not as individual Committee members.	**INDIVIDUAL**	1	2	3	4
	GROUP	1	2	3	4

COMMENTS:

2

TPS Norms and Beliefs Self- and Group-Assessment

HOW WE COMMUNICATE

INDICATORS	RATINGS				
1. It is our responsibility to set the tone for the entire school system, and we will make every effort to promote a positive image for our school system. The Superintendent will be visible in the community, and we will operate transparently and respectfully, maintain confidentiality, and respect the Open Meeting laws.	**INDIVIDUAL**	1	2	3	4
	GROUP	1	2	3	4
2. The Superintendent and the School Committee recognize the importance of proactive communication and agree that there will be no surprises. If School Committee members have questions or concerns, they agree to contact the Superintendent well in advance of a meeting.	**INDIVIDUAL**	1	2	3	4
	GROUP	1	2	3	4
3. We agree that discussion will be limited to the agenda, and items will not be added to the agenda unless it is determined by the Superintendent and the School Committee Chairperson that it would be detrimental to delay the issue until a subsequent meeting.	**INDIVIDUAL**	1	2	3	4
	GROUP	1	2	3	4
4. The Superintendent will share an annual planning calendar with School Committee members. If a member wishes to add an item to a future agenda, he or she should make a request to the Superintendent or the School Committee Chairperson. In turn, they will consult other members, as well as the annual planning calendar to gauge interest and alignment.	**INDIVIDUAL**	1	2	3	4
	GROUP	1	2	3	4
5. School Committee members agree to refer important questions and concerns they receive from members of the school community to the Superintendent. The Superintendent will investigate and provide all Committee members with the information needed to respond to an issue.	**INDIVIDUAL**	1	2	3	4
	GROUP	1	2	3	4
6. School Committee members will channel requests for information, reports, and data through the Superintendent and the School Committee Chair rather than directly to staff. The Superintendent will ensure that each member has equal access to this information.	**INDIVIDUAL**	1	2	3	4
	GROUP	1	2	3	4

TPS Norms and Beliefs Self- and Group-Assessment

7. The Superintendent intends to seek comprehensive solutions to problems and will create clear structures for decision making. In the spirit of continuous improvement, these structures may be revisited at any time.	**INDIVIDUAL**	1	2	3	4
	GROUP	1	2	3	4
8. The Superintendent and School Committee recognize the importance of working collaboratively with City officials to improve our schools, and we will actively seek ways to enlist their support in our efforts.	**INDIVIDUAL**	1	2	3	4
	GROUP	1	2	3	4

COMMENTS:

4

TPS Norms and Beliefs Self- and Group-Assessment

HOW WE IMPROVE

INDICATORS	RATINGS				
1. School Committee members and the Superintendent recognize the importance of professional growth and development, and they agree to participate in experiences designed to further their knowledge and understanding and to advance the work of the Taunton Public Schools.	**INDIVIDUAL**	1	2	3	4
	GROUP	1	2	3	4
2. In addition, School Committee members will participate in formal training organized by the Superintendent and the School Committee Chairperson and conducted by organizations such as the Massachusetts Association of School Committees (MASC) and/or Massachusetts Association of School Superintendents (MASS).	**INDIVIDUAL**	1	2	3	4
	GROUP	1	2	3	4
3. All new School Committee members will participate in an orientation session, and if desired, a School Committee mentor will be assigned.	**INDIVIDUAL**	1	2	3	4
	GROUP	1	2	3	4
4. The Superintendent and the School Committee agree to set aside time on an annual basis for self-evaluation and to review our progress toward adhering to agreed-upon norms and beliefs.	**INDIVIDUAL**	1	2	3	4
	GROUP	1	2	3	4
5. We recognize the importance of honoring our agreed-upon norms and beliefs, and we agree to take responsibility for reminding one another when we get off track.	**INDIVIDUAL**	1	2	3	4
	GROUP	1	2	3	4

COMMENTS:

5

TPS Self- and Group-Assessment Summary

Directions: Review and reflect upon the Norms and Beliefs under each category: (1) How We Govern; (2) How We Communicate; and (3) How We Improve. On a scale of 1 to 4 (1 being the lowest), rate your individual progress toward this indicator, as well as the progress of the group. If an indicator applies only to the Superintendent, it is not necessary to rate that indicator.

HOW WE GOVERN

INDICATORS		RESPONSES
1. We acknowledge that a School Committee is a meeting of the School Committee that is held in public—not a public meeting, and we will make every effort to ensure that Committee meetings are effective and efficient.	**AVERAGE** **GROUP**	3.25 3, 4, 3, 3, 4, 3, 3, 3
2. School Committee members agree to thoughtfully seek and support solutions that will provide the greatest benefit to students. Once the School Committee has taken action, Committee members will support the official position of the School Committee.	**AVERAGE** **GROUP**	3.375 4, 3, 3, 4, 3, 4, 3, 3
3. It is the responsibility of the Superintendent to oversee the hiring, evaluation, and handling of personnel issues; it is the responsibility of the School Committee to evaluate the Superintendent's effectiveness in these matters.	**AVERAGE** **GROUP**	3.125 3, 3, 4, 3, 3, 4, 2, 3
4. We acknowledge the importance of subcommittees, and the Superintendent agrees to utilize them to focus on a specific topic in-depth and to prepare for presentation, deliberation, and possible action by the full School Committee.	**AVERAGE** **GROUP**	2.285 2, 1, 2, N/A, 4, 2, 3, 2
5. School Committee members agree to recognize and respect that their authority exists when a quorum of the Committee meets and not as individual Committee members.	**AVERAGE** **GROUP**	3.375 3, 4, 3, 4, 3, 4, 3, 3

1

TPS Self- and Group-Assessment Summary

HOW WE COMMUNICATE

INDICATORS	RESPONSES	
1. It is our responsibility to set the tone for the entire school system, and we will make every effort to promote a positive image for our school system. The Superintendent will be visible in the community, and we will operate transparently and respectfully, maintain confidentiality, and respect the Open Meeting laws.	**AVERAGE** **GROUP**	3.428 4, 4, 3, N/A, 4, 3, 3, 3
2. The Superintendent and the School Committee recognize the importance of proactive communication and agree that there will be no surprises. If School Committee members have questions or concerns, they agree to contact the Superintendent well in advance of a meeting.	**AVERAGE** **GROUP**	2.875 3, 4, 3, 3, 3, 2, 2, 3
3. We agree that discussion will be limited to the agenda, and items will not be added to the agenda unless it is determined by the Superintendent and the School Committee Chairperson that it would be detrimental to delay the issue until a subsequent meeting.	**AVERAGE** **GROUP**	2.857 3, 3, 3, N/A, 3, 3, 2, 3
4. The Superintendent will share an annual planning calendar with School Committee members. If a member wishes to add an item to a future agenda, he or she should make a request to the Superintendent or the School Committee Chairperson. In turn, they will consult other members, as well as the annual planning calendar to gauge interest and alignment.	**AVERAGE** **GROUP**	3.00 N/A, N/A, 3, 3, 3, 4, 3, 2
5. School Committee members agree to refer important questions and concerns they receive from members of the school community to the Superintendent. The Superintendent will investigate and provide all Committee members with the information needed to respond to an issue.	**AVERAGE** **GROUP**	3.50 3, 4, 4, 4, 4, 3, 3, 3
6. School Committee members will channel requests for information, reports and data through the Superintendent and the School Committee Chair rather than directly to staff. The Superintendent will ensure that each member has equal access to this information.	**AVERAGE** **GROUP**	3.428 3, 4, 4, N/A, 4, 3, 3, 3

2

TPS Self- and Group-Assessment Summary

7. The Superintendent intends to seek comprehensive solutions to problems and will create clear structures for decision making. In the spirit of continuous improvement, these structures may be revisited at any time.	**AVERAGE**	3.40
	GROUP	3, N/A, N/A, 3, 4, 4, 3, N/A
8. The Superintendent and School Committee recognize the importance of working collaboratively with City officials to improve our schools, and we will actively seek ways to enlist their support in our efforts.	**AVERAGE**	3.571
	GROUP	3, 4, 3, N/A, 4, 4, 4, 3

3

TPS Self- and Group-Assessment Summary

HOW WE IMPROVE

INDICATORS	RESPONSES	
1. School Committee members and the Superintendent recognize the importance of professional growth and development, and they agree to participate in experiences designed to further their knowledge and understanding and to advance the work of the Taunton Public Schools.	**AVERAGE**	2.857
	GROUP	3, N/A, 3, 3, 3, 3, 3, 2
2. In addition, School Committee members will participate in formal training organized by the Superintendent and the School Committee Chairperson and conducted by organizations such as the Massachusetts Association of School Committees (MASC) and/or Massachusetts Association of School Superintendents (MASS).	**AVERAGE**	3.50
	GROUP	3, N/A, 3, N/A, 4, 4, 4, 3
3. All new School Committee members will participate in an orientation session, and if desired, a School Committee mentor will be assigned.	**AVERAGE**	3.666
	GROUP	N/A, N/A, N/A, 4, N/A, 4, 3
4. The Superintendent and the School Committee agree to set aside time on an annual basis for self-evaluation and to review our progress toward adhering to the agreed-upon norms and beliefs.	**AVERAGE**	3.285
	GROUP	4, N/A, 4, 3, 3, 3, 3, 3
5. We recognize the importance of honoring our norms and beliefs, and we agree to take responsibility for reminding one another when we get off track.	**AVERAGE**	2.75
	GROUP	2, 3, 3, 3, 4, 2, 2, 3

4

TAUNTON PUBLIC SCHOOLS

Julie Hackett, Ed.D.
Superintendent of Schools

215 Harris Street
Taunton, Massachusetts 02780
Tel. (508) 821-1100
Fax (508) 821-1177

Academic excellence for every student, in every classroom, in every school.

TPS Norms and Beliefs Pre-Work
March 14, 2012

Identify three (3) areas of strength in our work together and three (3) ways to improve our norms and beliefs. Note: A double asterisk (**) denotes comments submitted by the Superintendent.

Three Areas of Strength in Our Work Together

1. High Level of Respect/Trust
   - Pretty respectful of each other; even if we don't agree on things, we care about each other.
   - Lot of respect between people—whether you agree or not, we agree to disagree or agree to agree.
   - If somebody does make a comment, members don't blast the person for their remarks or beliefs.
   - Meetings are cordial for the most part, and members respect each other.
   - Even though we may not always agree, we trust and support one another through good times and bad (e.g., closure of schools, reductions-in-force).**
   - High level of trust among the group with the Superintendent.
   - SC appears to work together—a good working relationship.

2. Strong Communication
   - We keep the Superintendent informed; she keeps us informed.
   - When SC gets an issue from the community and passes it along, the Superintendent is always willing to follow up and talk to anyone in the community about their concerns.
   - We present a united front on issues—the public doesn't always like that because it's not what you see with other elected bodies.
   - SC members are the eyes and ears of the system, and they are always quick to give a "heads-up," keeping the Superintendent informed of issues in the community that may need to be addressed.**

3. A Focus on Students
   - Everybody cares about kids.
   - There is a great sense of pride in our school system; we believe in our students and staff and do our best to get them the very best (e.g., CTE classes, foreign language lab, field house floor, additional staff for inclusion, etc.).**

The Taunton Public School System does not discriminate on the basis of age, color, sex, religion, national origin, sexual orientation or disability.

Other

- The meetings are organized; the starting times and length of the meetings are going pretty well.
- Knowledgeable people from various backgrounds and interests serving on the committee.
- Obviously, appreciation of the hard work the Superintendent does, which suggests that when we want to make some changes, everyone should feel comfortable about raising those issues and concerns.
- The majority of the SC sincerely wants to improve and is willing to do what it takes to improve (but we're not exactly sure what that looks like or how to do it).

Three Ways to Improve Our Norms and Beliefs

1. "How We Govern"

Surprises during SC Meetings

- Sometimes SC members raise issues, and it feels like a "gotcha game" for the Superintendent and other SC members. SC members may support a subject that another member brings up, but the timing may not be right for whatever reason. The SC members are then between a rock and a hard spot because a vote is requested, which we may support, but the details are missing, so we appear uninformed.
- Subject matter is being brought up on the floor, and votes are being requested by other SC members without giving members time to look at the subject matter.
- If SC members have questions, they should be asked ahead of time.
- If something new comes up on the floor under new business, it might work better if it was referred to administration to see where it fits into the agenda items that are planned.
- Our current norms say that SC members will notify the Superintendent and Chair "well in advance" if they want items added to the agenda. This does not always happen, and there are times when motions are made on the floor to add items to the agenda (See "How We Communicate, #2, #3, and #4). This is problematic because it may be in conflict with the agendas being developed by the School Committee Chair and the Superintendent; it leaves little time to reflect upon and prioritize the request in relation to the approved goals. It can also feel like there are two separate agendas: one that the Superintendent and the Chair create together, and another to address the topics of interest for an individual member(s). **
- It may be helpful to further clarify what constitutes "new business." For example, it is helpful when SC members bring up under "new business" a burning issue in the community (e.g., community members are wondering about the installation of a new playground); it becomes tricky when "new business" includes the reading of a letter from a community member or a topic/item that an individual member wants to discuss. That said, there should be a way for SC members to publicly bring up their own ideas. **

Flexibility

- SC members could be more flexible in terms of scheduling meetings or changing dates.
- Think about holding the Norms and Beliefs Workshop at another time (maybe on a Saturday or Sunday?).

Role Clarity

- SC members are the Board of Directors and the Superintendent is the CEO, and we need to let her do her job.
- If a member makes a motion on the floor for an additional outside assignment, we need to be respectful of other members' and administrators' time.
- SC members should hold the Superintendent accountable to the agreed-upon outcomes identified in the goals submitted and approved by the School Committee; it would be helpful if the stylistic choices for how to get the work done were left to administration.
- Superintendents and SC members have a distinct set of roles and responsibilities; it may be helpful to clarify those. On the one hand, I want to be inclusive and involve others in the work that we do in the system, but at times that approach further diminishes role clarity. How do we strike a balance? **
- We need guidelines on our participation in the community—where should it extend and where should it stop? There are times when we may be overreaching our authority; individually, SC members can come out in favor or against anything they want.

2. "How We Communicate"
    - Improve wait time; no interruptions during reports, etc.
    - People tend to elaborate on issues and say the same thing over and over again; a simple "I tend to agree with so and so," or "I agree with the views that have been stated" would be helpful. At times it may appear that members of the SC are just looking for airtime or TV time.
    - Attack the issues, not the person.
    - Too many questions about small things that seem unimportant; feels nit-picky at times.
    - Limit snide remarks which seem harmless on the surface, yet could be taken personally.
    - Try to look at issues raised as new and separate from Taunton's issues in the past.
    - There needs to be a concerted effort on everyone's part to be a member of the team—that includes giving both good and bad news.
    - Everyone is capable of making a mistake; because we work with human beings and human beings are fallible, the right thing to do is to report issues right away to the Superintendent.

- If we don't work together as a team, we all start to look bad, and it can be detrimental to the system.
- E-mail—what's appropriate, and what isn't? Not clear that all of the items from the Superintendent are appropriate for e-mail (e.g., a change in the dates for SC meetings, the guidance around staff member's invitation, etc.).

3. "How We Improve"
    - Robert's Rules—not sure we are using them correctly.
    - Priorities—individual members have items that are of interest to them; some are raised during meetings, and some are raised outside of the meetings. As the Superintendent, I want to be responsive to all SC requests. I also have a set of approved goals to which I am held publicly accountable. More clarity on what is most important to the SC would be helpful. **
    - SC is still so committed to the past—we've always done it this way . . . we need to think differently about education, and radical change is needed.
    - SC is operating like a community that has no hope and we're doing what it takes to get by—how do we help our students advance?

APPENDIX 3.5 "My Burning Issue" Sample

"My Burning Issue" Sample

NAME: ***JANE DOE***

DIRECTIONS: In order to stay true to the core values in the Taunton Public Schools, from time to time it is important for us to review and reflect on problems that get in the way of our progress. Take a moment to identify an issue in our work together that you find the most challenging, and try to think about it from your colleagues' perspective. Identify possible solutions to address the problem.

MY BURNING ISSUE:

The issue that bothers me the most is . . . the way that we do Committee of the Whole/Subcommittee meetings now.

WHY IT BOTHERS ME:

- *I don't feel like a Chairperson of the Subcommittee anymore.*
- *It's confusing. Non-subcommittee members want to participate in the discussion, but only subcommittee members are allowed to vote on the issue.*
- *We have unintentionally diminished the role of the subcommittees in order to allow for full participation of other SC members.*
- *It's confusing to the public when all of us speak on the issue, but only a few of us vote.*
- *It's a Committee of the Whole meeting, but SC members don't always show up. How does this look to the public?*

WHAT MY COLLEAGUES MIGHT SAY ABOUT THIS:

- *We have to comply with the Open Meeting Law. SC members who are not part of a subcommittee can't sit at the table and participate under the OML unless we post as a Committee of the Whole.*
- *We need to decide what's more important—our traditional subcommittee structure or the opportunity for all SC members to participate in the discussion.*
- *If I am not on the subcommittee, how can I make an informed decision as a SC member if I don't have a chance to participate in the discussion?*

POSSIBLE SOLUTIONS:

- *Go back to the traditional way of doing subcommittees. Interested SC members can sit in the audience with the public.*
- *Eliminate subcommittees altogether.*

Find ways to make the new process clear to those participating and watching (e.g., Chair reads a statement at the beginning of the subcommittee to clarify the process).

TORCHH • TRUST • OPTIMISM • RESPECT FOR ALL • COLLABORATION • HIGH EXPECTATIONS • HARD WORK

Our core values [what we believe . . .]

TRUST: We believe that confidence in each other and a belief in each person's commitment to the educational process create the conditions necessary for children to grow and achieve.

OPTIMISM: We believe that vibrant educational environments foster student engagement and joyful learning and help to develop a positive outlook for all.

RESPECT FOR ALL: We believe in the importance of accepting and celebrating all human differences, and treating each student, family, and staff member with dignity and respect.

COLLABORATION: We believe that teamwork and partnerships are essential, and we are stronger and smarter together than we are alone.

HIGH EXPECTATIONS: We believe high academic standards keep us motivated and engaged, leading to higher levels of achievement.

HARD WORK: We believe that effective effort and a strong work ethic culminate in positive performance.

APPENDIX 3.6 "My Burning Issue" Blank Form

"My Burning Issue" Sample

NAME: *JANE DOE*

DIRECTIONS: In order to stay true to the core values in the Taunton Public Schools, from time to time it is important for us to review and reflect on problems that get in the way of our progress. Take a moment to identify an issue in our work together that you find the most challenging, and try to think about it from your colleagues' perspective. Identify possible solutions to address the problem.

TORCHH • TRUST • OPTIMISM • RESPECT FOR ALL • COLLABORATION • HIGH EXPECTATIONS • HARD WORK

MY BURNING ISSUE:

WHY IT BOTHERS ME:

WHAT MY COLLEAGUES MIGHT SAY ABOUT THIS:

POSSIBLE SOLUTIONS:

Our core values [what we believe . . .]

TRUST: We believe that confidence in each other and a belief in each person's commitment to the educational process create the conditions necessary for children to grow and achieve.

OPTIMISM: We believe that vibrant educational environments foster student engagement and joyful learning and help to develop a positive outlook for all.

RESPECT FOR ALL: We believe in the importance of accepting and celebrating all human differences, and treating each student, family, and staff member with dignity and respect.

COLLABORATION: We believe that teamwork and partnerships are essential, and we are stronger and smarter together than we are alone.

HIGH EXPECTATIONS: We believe high academic standards keep us motivated and engaged, leading to higher levels of achievement.

HARD WORK: We believe that effective effort and a strong work ethic culminate in positive performance.

APPENDIX 3.7 Ground Rules and Norms of Collaboration

GROUND RULES

- Be on time, be prepared, and stay involved.
- Be positive about the process.
- Take initiative and get clarification when needed.
- Check your air-time.
- Stay focused on the task.
- Be a leader and offer different solutions.
- Be courteous, open-minded, and respectful of the point of view of others.

NORMS OF COLLABORATION

1. **Pausing** – Slows down the "to and fro" of discussion.
2. **Paraphrasing**– Re-casts or translates into one's own words; to summarize or to provide an example of what has just been said.
3. **Probing for Specificity** – Probing seeks to clarify something which is not yet fully understood.
4. **Putting Ideas on the Table** – It takes a degree of self-confidence and courage to put forward an idea, and it is vital that collaborative groups nurture such self-confidence and courage.
5. **Paying Attention to Self and Others** – Collaborative work is facilitated when each team member is explicitly conscious of self and others - not only aware of what he or she is saying, but also how it is said and how others are responding to it.
6. **Presuming Positive Intentions** – This is the assumption that other members of the team are acting from positive and constructive intentions, however much we may disagree with their ideas.
7. **Pursuing a Balance between Advocacy and Inquiry** – Highly effective teams are aware of the necessity of inquiry and advocacy and self-consciously attempt to balance them.

Love, N., Stiles, K., and Mundry, S., eds. *A Data Coach's Guide to Improving Learning for All Students*. Thousand Oaks: Corwin Press, 2008.

APPENDIX 3.8 Norms Retreat Agenda Example

AGENDA

Location: Elizabeth Pole School

School Committee Retreat
TPS NORMS AND BELIEFS
February 12, 2014
6:00–9:00 p.m.

Anticipated Outcomes:

1. An opportunity for new members to weigh in on our norms and beliefs;
2. A chance to reflect on our progress to date and explore ways we can strengthen our team.

Time	Item
6:00–6:10 p.m.	**History/Overview**
6:10–6:30 p.m.	**Agenda, Ground Rules, 7 Norms of Collaboration**
6:30–6:45 p.m.	**Activity #1: Why I Love Being on the TPS Team!** • It's easy to talk about what's wrong, but much harder to talk about what's right. For the next 15 minutes, let's focus on the positives. • Jot down three ideas/reasons about why you love being on the TPS Team. Think about what's working and how our work together makes a difference.
6:45–8:45 p.m.	**Activity #2: My Burning Issues Protocol** Ideas have been submitted for ways that we can do a better job with communication, governance, and improving as a team. We will use the following process to address some of your most pressing concerns and update our norms and beliefs document: • Frame the Problem (1 minute)—Julie will frame each issue in the context of norms and beliefs; • State the Problem (5 minutes)—each SC member explains his/her issue in his/her own words, and shares why it's a concern for them (all other members listen); • Colleague Feedback (10 minutes)—School Committee members will ask questions about their colleague's issue, give input on how they view the problem, and make suggestions for how to address it (speaker listens); • Speaker States Next Steps (3 minutes)—After hearing the input from my colleagues, here's what I think should happen next . . . • Consensus (1 minute)—Survey the group to determine if there is consensus on the Speaker's next steps.
8:45–9:00 p.m.	**Summary of Our Progress Tonight/Next Steps**

AGENDA

School Committee Workshop
October 10, 2011
4:00–8:30 p.m.

Purpose
When dedicated educational leaders understand that students are the primary focus, we get high performing schools. In an effort to lead by example, the Taunton School Committee made a formal commitment in 2009 to conduct biannual workshops designed to give the Superintendent and the School Committee an opportunity to focus on how we work together and how we can improve. This is the first of two workshops we will have this year to review and reflect upon our "norms and beliefs."

Pre-Work
All participants are asked to carefully review the Taunton Norms and Beliefs and complete the self-assessment. Data will be collected and compiled in advance of the workshop. You are asked to share your self4 assessment with the Superintendent and/or the School Committee Chairperson by no later than Tuesday, October 9, 2011.

Anticipated Outcomes:
1. Reflect upon our individual and group progress to date;
2. Revise and reaffirm the "TPS Norms and Beliefs";
3. Develop consensus on annual School Committee topics;
4. Consider the Superintendent's evaluation tool and the strategic priorities for goals.

Time	Item(s)
4:00–4:30 p.m.	Tour of the Hall of Fame
4:45–5:00 p.m.	Review Purpose, Agenda, and Outcomes
5:00–6:00 p.m.	Norms and Beliefs Activity—review the self-assessment data to determine areas of strength and opportunities for improvement for each one of the three categories: • How We Govern (20 minutes) • How We Communicate (20 minutes) • How We Improve (20 minutes)
6:00–7:00 p.m.	*Working Dinner*
7:00–8:15 p.m.	Evaluation Process for Superintendent of Schools • Review current process • Review DESE process • Identify preferred evaluation tool • Consensus on priority areas of focus for goals
8:15–8:30 p.m.	Reflections—participants will have an opportunity to reflect upon the conversation, and share personal insights by responding to the following: *"As a result of our work together this evening, I have more clarity on . . ."*

CHAPTER FOUR

Establishing a Collective Vision with Strategic Planning

Having a well-articulated strategy helps leaders choose what to do and, just as importantly, what not to do. As a result, the organization can put its scarce resources to use more effectively.

—CHILDRESS ET AL., 2007

IF YOU HANDED ANY GROUP in your school community—students, parents, teachers, staff, or school board—a piece of paper and a few markers, asking them to draw *your* vision for their school system, would they be able to do it? What images would you hope to see? Your vision may be of smiling graduates in caps and gowns heading to top-tier colleges and landing impressive jobs. Your preferred future for your students might evoke a picture of empty lines at food banks and children who have grown into happy, healthy, well-educated adults, gainfully employed and putting an end to generational poverty and hunger. Democracy might be the theme of the hopes and dreams for your children with a focus on teaching your graduates—particularly young men of color and young women of all races—to exercise their right to vote and run for elections, serving on local school boards, city councils, and in the highest offices in the state

A COLLECTIVE VISION WITH STRATEGIC PLANNING

MATERIALS NEEDED

- Entry interview data
- Student achievement data
- Former strategic plans

THE PROCESS

1. Plan on your own terms.
2. Develop the architecture of your strategic plan.
   - Create core values.
   - Make a mission.
   - Develop a vision.
   - Establish strategic priorities.
3. Create a draft strategic plan.
4. Engage stakeholders.
5. Gather data and identify challenges.
6. Assemble a synthesis team.
7. Talk it up.
8. Get results.

and the nation. All superintendents should have a well-articulated vision for their students, and the confidence to know that it will be understood by members of their school community.

While every school leader should have a vision, it is not always the case that every one does, and this can negatively impact superintendent–school board relationships. The great philosopher Seneca once said, "If one doesn't know to which port one is sailing, any wind is favorable."[1] It is the unfortunate truth that often any wind will do for the hard-charging reformer, eager to unveil his latest, greatest scheme for educational improvements, but far less enthusiastic about putting effort into the conventions of collaboration. This type of reform is typically accompanied by lots of flash, fanfare, and fancy-sounding titles like "Operation Achieve" or "Project Pathway to Success." With little substance or thought behind their effort and some sleight of hand, these school reformers pretend that the changes will be the answer to all of the district's challenges. They discount the many other initiatives that were previously rolled out, pretending they no longer require any effort from educators or school boards, drawing all attention to this latest reform soon to become another layer in the initiative panacea for underperforming schools.[2]

High-profile school reforms like these (especially those with little substance or relevance) tend to leave the school board and school community on the outside looking in because they are too leader-centric and singularly focused to build productive teams. The playbooks that are rolled out are cut and pasted from scripted reform efforts driven by outside influences that have little or no connection to the school community in question. School board members and others do not understand the leader's vision, if there is one, and they play only minor cameos in the reform effort or have no role at all. This kind of school reformer gets the attention he needs, making an "above the fold" splash to position himself well for his next job, but initiative churn soon creeps in, leaving the school board and educators dazed, confused, and uncertain about their school district's priorities. Establishing a collective vision through strategic planning helps superintendents, school boards, and school community members own the work and commit to the complex efforts involved in creating strategic plans that lead to better opportunities for students.

There is no greater threat to a relationship than the miscommunication that can result in the absence of a clearly articulated plan for the future. And there is no greater opportunity for you to build stronger bonds with members of your school board and school community than by leading the strategic planning efforts in your school system. Teaching the school system about the elements of a strategic plan and facilitating the process that leads to its creation present an ideal opportunity for you when you see your role as a lead teacher responsible for helping your organization learn and grow. From core values to a collective vision, when you assume responsibility for strategic planning, you build stronger relationships with members of your school board and school community, ensuring a clear path for the dedication of resources and a clear direction for the district.

Strategic plans matter for a school system and its students. The question of whether such plans are a meaningful undertaking for you can best be answered by what happens when you, the school board, and school community members are only superficially involved in the process. When a school community has not been given an opportunity to engage in careful planning, tensions mount and people make up their own rules. A teacher confused about which curriculum to use will use one that makes the most sense to him. A principal unclear about the district's expectations for student learning will evaluate teachers the best way she knows how. A school board member confused about the importance of foreign language in the elementary schools may not support your budgetary increase for additional foreign language teachers. If classroom teachers, building principals, and school board members have to guess what matters most and why, the outcomes are unpredictable and relationships can quickly become strained.

Leading a school system unclear on its priorities is a challenge to be sure. As a school leader who has spearheaded a number of strategic planning initiatives for nonprofits and school districts throughout New England, I have witnessed the pressures and sources of confusion that arise in the absence of a strategic plan. In one school system during the entry-plus process, I listened to school board and school community members who had worked with no strategic plan for a number of years, and many unanswered questions rose to the surface. Do we want a comprehensive high school with more career technical education courses, or is it best to leave that to the regional vocational schools? Is it important for us to explore inclusionary models of learning, or should we continue to outsource services for our students with special needs? Should technology-based instructional practices in the classroom be mandated, or do we still value traditional approaches to teaching and learning? These unanswered questions are the result of what I call "initiative churn," a phrase borrowed from Elmore's "policy churn,"[3] which means the premature implementation of new projects in the school system when there is a lack of clarity about the district's collective beliefs. When expectations for the school community are unclear, there is a level of chaos and confusion in the school system that can be dramatically improved with a well-thought-out strategic plan.

WHY SUPERINTENDENTS SHOULD TAKE THE LEAD

Superintendents who are the best educational leaders view themselves as teachers of an enormous classroom, eager to instruct their students—an attentive legion of educators, school community, and school board members. If you could dream up the perfect lesson for a superintendent of schools to teach to her oversized class, no content could be more appropriate than showing your "students" how to establish core values, a mission, a vision, and strategic priorities. Strategic planning gives you an opportunity to clarify your priorities and shape the future, setting a clear pathway for student success to help you build and solidify relationships with your school board and school community.

Setting the course or a vision for a school system is widely considered the work of superintendents, so it makes sense for you to take a more active role in leading this effort. While it is true that the demands on superintendents have increased exponentially in the last few years,[4] when you are working with your school board to develop a relationship-building mindset, taking a lead role in strategic planning can be powerful. These days it is not uncommon for school leaders to pay tens of thousands of dollars to hire someone to oversee and coordinate the strategic planning process, which is understandable given the ever-increasing expectations for superintendents. These leaders hire consultants to obtain and organize data, communicate the plan, get input from various stakeholders, manage personalities, and produce elaborate written documents that signify the completion of the strategic planning effort. The problem with this model is that you are less likely to be intimately involved in the work, which means you are less familiar with the elements of the plan—and more importantly, the concepts that your school board and school community truly wish to convey. When all is said and done, the strategic plan becomes something separate and apart from the work you do, and it is relegated to a pile of old relics on a dusty shelf.

When it comes to relationship building, an opportunity is lost when you separate yourself from the strategic planning effort. If you are only marginally involved in the work, is it any wonder that some strategic plans outlive their usefulness? As superintendent, you are more likely to use the strategic plan in a variety of contexts if you are more conversant with its contents. If you are intimately involved in the process of accumulating data, interpreting progress, and utilizing the strategic plan in a variety of contexts, you will be more inclined to align aspects of your work, including the budget, your speeches, and other actions and forms of communication, to the strategic plan.

I can appreciate that you might find the strategic planning process daunting because it is sometimes hard to get the words just right—it might seem impossible to even know how to begin—but you can always work out the technical details with your administrative team or others you trust. In relationship-building, conversations are critically important, and the school community's view of your role in these discussions can provide valuable insight into your school board's thought process, simultaneously strengthening connections. Taking the lead on strategic planning efforts signifies that you are an accessible leader of a school system, and you are willing to roll up your sleeves and work directly with stakeholders and the school board.

If the thought of this effort makes you a little weak in the knees, it may be helpful to know that you can take either a more active or passive role in the strategic planning, and both approaches will likely give your school community a sense of direction. When you are the person charged with establishing a vision for your school community, leading the strategic planning effort presents a natural opportunity for you to demonstrate your teaching skills and forge connections with your school board and school community. If you find you need more support, you can hire a consultant to help you frame the process, but you are still encouraged to take the lead if you want to strengthen your superintendent–school board relations. If you are a leader who is more confident in the role of teacher, thinking about strategic planning as a series of lessons may be helpful. There are several important steps you can follow in the strategic planning process to help you set a clear course for your school system and establish stronger ties to your school board and school community.

THE STRATEGIC PLANNING PROCESS

Every strategic planning process generally includes an overview of the development of the plan, a method for enlisting stakeholders, a strategy to gather data, and a particular way to craft and communicate the elements of the plan. This approach to strategic planning gets the job done, and the documents that are produced are technically accurate and grammatically correct. However, this book is about building relationships, so I am going to share several ways you can focus your attention on deepening your school board relationships as you work through the strategic planning process.

I have led many strategic planning efforts in various organizations, finding it necessary to customize the approach to meet the needs of the particular non-profit or school system, and no one process I have used has been exactly the same. For example, in one school district, the strategic planning efforts were directed almost exclusively by the school board. In another school system, the high school was pursuing accreditation, so educators at the secondary level happened to be the most intimately involved and invested in the strategic planning because it was relevant to their other efforts. Context is everything in strategic planning and relationship building, and I cannot emphasize strongly enough the role that it plays in the recommended strategies in this book or how vitally important it is for you to have a sense for what will and will not work in your own school system or organization.

As the lead architect of your district's strategic plan, you have a chance to interact with many stakeholders on a frequent basis, which is where the relationship-building opportunities come into play. When I decided to lead the strategic planning process as a superintendent to get maximum buy-in and support from my school board, I supplemented traditional strategic planning processes with these steps: (1) plan on your own terms; (2) develop the architecture of your strategic plan; (3) create a draft strategic plan; (4) engage stakeholders; (5) gather data and identify challenges; (6) assemble a synthesis team; (7) talk it up; and (8) get results. The end result is a strategic plan that helped us establish a collective vision and priorities to which we are all committed and outcomes for our students in which we can all take pride.

Step 1: Plan on Your Own Terms

There are many ways to approach strategic planning, and there is no one way to get the job done. The first step in the process is to determine how you will define the elements of your strategic plan. Some define the architecture of a strategic plan one way including core values, a mission, a vision, strategic priorities, and goals; whereas others leave out strategic priorities and create goals, objectives, and action steps instead. Some, like Olsen and Olsen, define vision as "the specific mountain you are currently trying to climb—the where,"[5] and others say it is like a crystal ball where you see into the future and get a glimpse of what your schools will look like ten years from now. Superintendents may be intimidated by the technical aspects of strategic planning, but no matter how you decide to structure your plan, the elements you choose to teach are far less important than the process itself. Communicating to others how you plan to lead the process and why the work is important is job one, and if you do this up front, you establish your intentions and solidify your role as the lead teacher in the effort.

With every strategic planning process I have led, in nearly every case at least one person on the board has had substantial strategic planning experience, typically in the private or nonprofit sectors. Dealing with such experience can be intimidating at first, but you should view it as the perfect opportunity to get to know this board member better and tap into her expertise. Asking a school board member for her input on the architecture of the strategic plan can be a useful way to honor her knowledge and skills and involve that person in the strategic planning effort.

A word of caution: potential pitfalls can arise if other school board members think that one member is setting the course for the entire school board and district. By establishing yourself as the clear leader in this process—one who is willing to collaborate and take input from all board members, including those who have expertise in this area—you will build trust in the strategic planning effort and gain the confidence of your school board members.

Step 2: Develop the Architecture of Your Strategic Plan

In the next step, I develop a timeline for creating the strategic plan, and in presentations, televised meetings, and written correspondence, I communicate the many ways school community members can get involved. I then begin to teach the architecture of the strategic plan we will be creating, containing the main elements: core values, a mission, a vision, and strategic priorities. These elements are important because they provide the framework for the conditions of an effective organization. Exhibit 4.1 is an excerpt from a PowerPoint presentation I created to help my school board and school community understand the architecture of a strategic plan and my approach to the process. I shared this

EXHIBIT 4.1 The architecture of a strategic plan

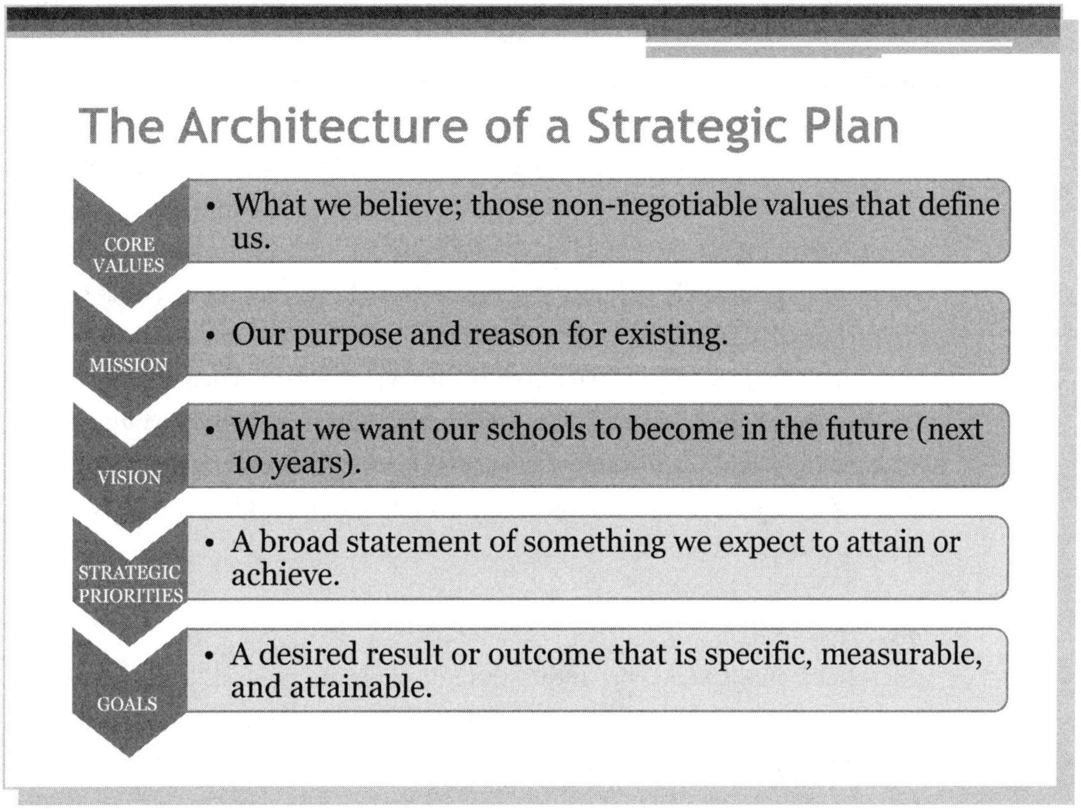

presentation shortly after we completed our norms and beliefs to generate interest with various groups (i.e., the school board, administrators, synthesis team, and others).

Create Core Values

The first component of a strategic plan is the core values. I find it easier to begin with the core values because school board and school community members generally have a sense of the beliefs that are most important to their culture. Using the superintendent–school board norms and beliefs protocol can be helpful in this process. Core values relate to the morals and ethics of the district, and while school systems may hold beliefs similar to others (for example, *trust* tends to be a universal core value), a good set of core values will also reflect the unique characteristics of those in your school system. In my school district, the slogan "where hard work prevails" was used for years. Over time, many who lived and grew up in the system worked their way up through the ranks, earning promotions by staying late many nights and giving up their weekends. Historically, those who have been "clock watchers," new to the system and eager to punch out at the end of the school day, have had more difficulty assimilating into our culture. In other places I have worked, staying late in the office was not valued nearly as much and may even have been considered an inefficient practice (e.g., "you wouldn't need to stay late if you knew how to delegate and focused on the task at hand"). Hard work is an unspoken expectation in my school system, which is why we made sure to include it as one of our core values.

Make a Mission

When I talk about a mission in the strategic planning process, I like to define it as an organization's purpose or reason for existing. What does your school system or organization do that no one else's does? Together, my school board and I determined that our mission, or our reason for existing, is to make certain that every child, regardless of strengths or limitations, experiences academic success. Our mission is "academic excellence for every student, in every classroom, in every school," and it is one in which we now all believe. I find it easier to begin with the organization's mission or purpose rather than vision because it helps to know your organization's reason for existing when it comes time to dream up future possibilities for your school district and students. Our discussions around mission also make it easier to recognize, for instance, that when we create programs for students with special needs—students who are gifted in many ways, but for whom academics may be a challenge—we also need to consider opportunities for those students who excel academically.

Develop a Vision

The vision can be the most difficult for the synthesis team to create because educators are all too often saddled with self-imposed limitations that come from public expectations, laws and mandates, and limited resources. If the mind wanders to how difficult something will be to implement, the natural inclination may be to avoid the topic. Previously, I mentioned early exposure to foreign languages; this is but one example of an element in the vision that caused great consternation for synthesis team members. They liked the idea of giving students more opportunities, but we were an urban school system facing a multimillion dollar deficit and school closures—to even think about what it would take to implement elementary foreign languages in the face of cuts and closures seemed impractical. After much debate, we kept this proposal in our vision, as you will see in our finalized strategic plan in appendix 4.1. Resources are still an issue, but we committed to finding ways to expand foreign languages when we developed the strategic plan; as a result, we now offer foreign languages to all eighth graders with plans in the early stages of development to expand to all elementary schools.

Establish Strategic Priorities

An optional step in the process is the development of strategic priorities or overarching goals. These are the aspects of the strategic plan to which school leaders and employees in the school system can attach their commitments and pledges. We used a total of four strategic priorities in our strategic plan, and the superintendent, central office administrators, school-based administrators, and educators derived their goals and action steps from this list. The four strategic priorities include (1) Post-Secondary Pursuits—We will work continuously to improve student achievement and prepare all learners for successful post-secondary pursuits; (2) Personalization—We will create safe, inclusive, and personalized learning environments for all students; (3) Communication—We will develop clear and effective forms of communication to enhance teaching and learning; and (4) Resources—We will maximize our resources of time, talent, and finances. Each of these strategic priorities provides an important framework to situate the goals, action steps, and the work we do on a day-to-day basis. I go into more depth on how the superintendent can develop district goals that are derived from strategic priorities in chapter 5.

Step 3: Create a Draft Strategic Plan

Next, I begin to develop a draft based on my own reflections about school community members' hopes and dreams for the future. This draft should include possible core values, a mission, a vision, and strategic priorities. I find it helpful to put pen to paper and make the first draft of the strategic plan myself, but I recognize that I happen to be someone who enjoys this type of activity. If writing is a task you would rather avoid, enlist a talented member of your synthesis team to develop a first draft. Finalizing strategic plans can take an eternity because each stakeholder comes to the table with a different set of experiences and values, so getting in place a workable draft that can be tweaked is a useful way to get started.

Step 4: Engage Stakeholders

Engaging a group of stakeholders in the strategic planning process is important to the usefulness and accessibility of the plan. If your goal is to develop a plan that reflects the values of your school community, then hearing as many voices as possible is critical to its success. Make a chart showing all the different people, groups, and organizations that have a stake in your school system, and identify who might be the most effective ambassadors in the process. A logical way to do this is to go back to your entry-plus plan to determine group representation in the strategic planning and get input from your school board about the types of people who might be good partners in the process. In my case, I talked about the strategic planning process during televised meetings, and disseminated information about it and ways that individuals could get involved at these televised school board meetings, administrative meetings, on our Web site, and through e-mail blasts. Another good way to get those who are not directly involved in the strategic planning effort to participate is to create surveys and feedback loops in which synthesis team members share strategic planning drafts with constituents. For example, a mathematics curriculum supervisor serving on the synthesis team may take the draft back to her colleagues in the math department for their consideration. Other synthesis team members can also obtain input from their colleagues who share similar roles (and those who do not), bringing any important information back to the team for consideration.

I have created strategic plans that I developed strictly with the school board and others I developed with a more diverse group of stakeholders in a synthesis team. Both approaches work well, but school board input is critical either way. During those times when I worked with the synthesis team, I asked the school board to vote and appoint a couple of designees to serve as members, and these individuals worked directly with the team to help refine the ideas and language. It is important that no school board members feel excluded from this process, particularly when your primary purpose is to strengthen relationships. In an effort to be more inclusive, I made sure that my school board knew I would be using the data and information they had shared with me during our entry-plus interviews and norms and beliefs discussions to inform the strategic plan. For example, after much discussion and debate, we decided including elementary foreign languages in the vision was something we could all support. In addition, I kept all school board members apprised of our progress throughout the strategic planning efforts by including regular updates in my superintendent's reports, sharing drafts of the plan in various stages of development, and asking for their input on different aspects of the plan.

Step 5: Gather Data and Identify Challenges

If you have been following the relationship-building progression in this book, you already have a set of data and information you can use based on what you learned from your entry-plus and norms and beliefs work. In that work you embedded questions to address core values, a mission, a vision, and strategic priorities, and you can use this information to generate ideas to get you started. You should also think about other sources of information that you can use to craft the district's strategic plan. Documents might include past strategic plans, other mission statements, accreditation documents, your strategic priorities, demographic data, capital improvement and other plans, student achievement results, historical information about your municipality and school system, and possibly superintendent evaluation documents.

I read through all this information and start to write notes to myself about important elements to include in the strategic plan. On one page I capture ideas or important words from my document analysis that might inform our core values. On another page, I capture feelings or beliefs about the school system that can be part of a ten-year vision. I repeat this process for the mission and strategic priorities. Next, I identify areas of concern that need to be addressed in the next five years.

Step 6: Assemble a Synthesis Team

Once I have mapped out my own thoughts and ideas about the various elements of the strategic plan, I then assemble a synthesis team, introducing them to the same process I used previously (see step 5). The synthesis team can be composed of the school board members alone or members of a more diverse group of stakeholders. If your school board wants to take the lead in this work, it is a good idea for you to support this effort, but be sure to develop agendas and post strategic planning sessions as public meetings, incorporating many opportunities for school community input. This can make the process more complex because public meetings mean that school board members' ideas can be challenged at an early stage when they are not yet ripe. I find that public meetings, in this case, can make school board members more guarded and less likely to "dream big" for fear of scrutiny or reprisal by an already skeptical public. For this reason, I prefer to work with a more diverse group of stakeholders that may include some of the critics, as well as representatives of the school board.

The synthesis team members then generate their own ideas in a carousel activity in much the same way I generated my own thoughts and ideas about the elements of the strategic plan. This can be done by posting large paper around the room, displaying your strategic planning architecture (i.e., core values, a mission, a vision, and strategic priorities). Individual synthesis team members can then add their ideas to each concept on the chart paper until you have a collection of words and phrases representing a particular element of the strategic plan. Finally, synthesis team members can use stickers or a check-mark process to highlight or flag those ideas that resonate most with them. Soon, you will have a prioritized, brainstormed collection of ideas for every element of your strategic plan.

As you begin to develop the draft, you may find that even the most articulate members of your synthesis team get stymied in the strategic planning process because they get stuck on the wording for a particular idea. I emphasize that the concepts are what is most important at this juncture, not the words. I then take the pressure off the synthesis team by working with a few wordsmiths, a smaller group of four or five individuals (including at least one school board member), that I task with helping me write drafts and make the elements of the strategic plan fit together coherently. These drafts are always subject to the approval of the synthesis team and ultimately the school board, and typically the drafts go through several iterations before they are finalized. Sharing these drafts regularly with the school board helps foster a sense of ownership and trust important in relationship building.

Step 7: Talk It Up

Quite by accident, in the last strategic plan I facilitated for a school system, we developed core values that I was able to assemble into a TORCHH acronym: Trust, Optimism, Respect, Collaboration, Hard Work, and High Achievement. Although I would never recommend that you start with a catchy mnemonic device and back into the core values, in this case the acronym is useful because it enables us to use the core values more widely; very often conversations that involve student discipline or personnel issues will harken back to these TORCHH core values. We also frame the conversations at new teacher orientations around our core values to signal to our newcomers who we are and what values define us. In addition, we enlisted our talented graphic arts students, one of whom created the design you see in exhibit 4.2. We call this the "TORCHH symbol," which contains our school system's core values. We use it on letterhead,

EXHIBIT 4.2 TORCHH symbol

bookmarks, notepads, signage, and the table skirts that are used at formal school board meetings.

Step 8: Get Results

I was able to use the data from the entry-plus process to identify problems and acknowledge widespread community concerns. For example, I learned about the special education financial issues in entry-plus and addressed them through strategic planning efforts, building the support I needed to make changes that transformed our school system. The overidentification of students with special needs was a significant issue; there were a disproportionate number of students of color in substantially separate settings and rarely an occasion for students to return to the general educational setting. We put two additional special education administrators in place, ensuring students were properly identified for special education services. This new organizational structure, with the two additional administrators, has helped to save the system many times over the cost of their combined salaries because we have established better oversight and controls on spending. For example, students are no longer assigned to an out-of-district placement unless the data support such a placement. We were also able to significantly reduce outplacement costs by eliminating the number of one-on-one educational assistants for students whose educational needs required a less restrictive environment and more independence. We later built our own in-district programs and appropriately staffed them for students with special needs, decreasing the number of outplacements, reducing exorbitant costs, and increasing students' opportunities for inclusion.

Strategic planning represents a golden opportunity for you to paint your future as the lead teacher in your district, working together with school board and school community members to form a collective vision for your schools. You can outsource the work to a consultant who can lead the charge, and the process may still provide your school system with the direction it needs to make a difference for students—but you may lose out on important relationship-building opportunities. If you are serious about strengthening your relationship with the school board, you may want to consider the ways in which strategic planning can establish your leadership, creating opportunities for you to learn more about your school community and ways to help your students improve. A superintendent who takes the lead on strategic planning will never be asked by the school board or school community what it is that she wants most for the children she serves.

APPENDIX 4.1 TPS Strategic Plan

TAUNTON PUBLIC SCHOOLS STRATEGIC PLAN

Our Mission [what we do] . . .

Academic excellence for every student, in every classroom, in every school.

Vision [where we see ourselves in ten years . . .]

Taunton Public Schools is a leader amongst schools in the Commonwealth and throughout the nation. Our students will benefit from a comprehensive world-class education marked by innovative educational practices that prepare each one for a productive life in a global society. Academic excellence extends beyond traditional intellectual pursuits to provide a gateway to a better life.

Students will flourish within an environment that includes:

- Safe, well-maintained, and aesthetically pleasing schools.
- Educators who are outstanding role models and collaborate to create inclusive and engaging learning environments.
- Personalized instruction that is tailored to meet the educational needs of every student.
- Early exposure to foreign languages, health and wellness, music and the arts.
- Technology that is fully and effectively integrated with learning.

The Taunton School District teaches our students the values and skills necessary to succeed in a diverse and ever-changing global society. We strive to create an atmosphere of high expectations and joyful learning, where students are encouraged to work together, take academic risks, think critically, and pursue successful careers and higher education. We give our students the knowledge and experiences they need to live happy, healthy, and productive lives.

Strategic Priorities

1—POST-SECONDARY PURSUITS: We will work to continuously improve student achievement and to prepare all learners for successful post-secondary pursuits.

2—PERSONALIZATION: We will create safe, inclusive, and personalized learning environments for all students.

3—COMMUNICATION: We will develop clear and effective forms of communication to enhance teaching and learning.

4—RESOURCES: We will maximize our resources of time, talent, and finances.

Our core values [what we believe . . .]

TRUST: We believe that confidence in each other and a belief in each person's commitment to the educational process create the conditions necessary for children to grow and achieve.

OPTIMISM: We believe that vibrant educational environments foster student engagement and joyful learning and help to develop a positive outlook for all.

RESPECT FOR ALL: We believe in the importance of accepting and celebrating all human differences, and treating each student, family, and staff member with dignity and respect.

COLLABORATION: We believe that teamwork and partnerships are essential, and we are stronger and smarter together than we are alone.

HIGH EXPECTATIONS: We believe high academic standards keep us motivated and engaged, leading to higher levels of achievement.

HARD WORK: We believe that effective effort and a strong work ethic culminate in positive performance.

CHAPTER FIVE

Turning Vision into Reality: Inclusive Goal Setting

In districts with higher levels of student achievement, the local board of education is aligned with and supportive of the non-negotiable goals for achievement and instruction. They ensure these goals remain the primary focus of the district's efforts and that no other initiatives detract attention or resources from accomplishing these goals.

—WATERS & MARZANO, 2006

WITH A RELENTLESS FOCUS on goals that matter, a school board can be a powerful catalyst for change. School boards that exercise the right amount of pressure and support to attain district goals create productive superintendent–school board teams. I once led strategic planning efforts for a superintendent and school board who were focused on not just reducing—but eliminating—achievement gaps for children of color. The school board in this high performing district unanimously adopted two goals (1) eliminate the achievement gap, and (2) foster a cycle of continuous improvement using data, and board members took this work seriously. School board presentations were devoted to these topics and little else;

even when a presentation was unrelated, the school board made it so by viewing everything through an "achievement gap" lens.

I remember a school board meeting when the athletic director gave his annual school board presentation on student athletic participation. He shared data showing how student participation in athletics had substantially increased in the district over time. The school board appreciated that more students were involved in healthy activities and connected to their schools, but they were even more interested in the participation rates of students of color. They wanted to know if the athletic director could share whether the proportion of students of color in various sports mirrored the population of students of color in the district. The athletic director explained why it would be a challenge to apply this standard to athletics, and the school board nodded, smiled politely, and gave examples of how it could and would be done.

This exchange was most impressive because it was not the focus of a school board member or two—*every* board member considered it his or her obligation to remain vigilant about the district goals. Throughout the strategic planning process, they worked with their superintendent to gain consensus, developing inclusive goals that would challenge everyone in the district—including themselves. There is no better way to strengthen superintendent–school board relationships than by working together to solve complex and challenging problems that will help students achieve

THE INCLUSIVE GOAL-SETTING PROCESS

MATERIALS NEEDED

- Entry plan
- Norms and beliefs
- Strategic plan
- Superintendent's self-evaluation
- Goals from previous years

THE PROCESS

1. Frontloading—Use goal reflections to prepare your school board for high-impact goals.
2. Identifying possible goals—Consider your own priorities, as well as those of your school board, and generate a "goal possibilities list" of ideas; ask school board members for input.
3. Drafting goals—Create draft goals and check in with school board members to see whether you have captured their ideas.
4. Communicating progress toward goal attainment—Give the school board frequent updates on your progress toward goals to gain their trust and confidence.

more. The highest performing school districts, like the "moving districts" described in the early chapters of this book, are those with superintendents and school boards who collaborate and gain consensus on non-negotiable student achievement goals, allowing nothing to stand in the way of attaining their hopes and dreams for the children they serve.

Goal attainment is beneficial to students, and collaboration helps you and your school board derive a greater sense of purpose and meaning from your work. Bonds are strengthened even more when the focus of your work is to overcome impediments to student success. It may be counterintuitive for you to set the conditions for holding your own feet to the fire, but if you are serious about changing your school system for the better, an important partner in this process is your school board. You may be a superintendent who has effectively implemented norms and beliefs and a thoughtful strategic plan, but you may still feel uncertain about the best way to construct meaningful goals that your school board will support. In what ways can you and the school board work together to develop a set of goals? How do you show respect for your school board's priorities and accomplish the work that you believe to be most important? And is there a way for you to come to agreement with the school board about what work is most important for your students?

Inclusive goal setting requires superintendent–school board teamwork and an unrelenting focus on making your collective vision for students a reality. You can use the inclusive goal-setting process to get results, deepening your sense of camaraderie with the school board in the process. I have seen inclusive goal setting result in many positive changes for students, including increases in student acceptances to top colleges, increases in the number of students graduating from high school, and significant decreases in the number of students dropping out of school. Cultivating this type of collaborative culture and a deliberate goal-setting process creates better opportunities and outcomes for students, enabling you and your school board to engage in challenging reforms.

Next, I will share with you how my school board and I used this process to cut the dropout rate in half, creating better opportunities for our students who need them most. The inclusive goal-setting process has led to a cultural shift in the way that we think about students who are at risk of dropping out of school. Thanks to the efforts of many, students are not a statistic; they are real people with names, faces, and personal stories—they are sons, daughters, brothers, and sisters who have encountered obstacles in life and deserve a happy ending. There is a greater awareness and appreciation for these children and their experiences now, and this shift means that our expectations have increased. Many of the at-risk students who were once not expected to graduate from high school now earn a diploma and go on to college. These efforts also have deepened superintendent–school board relations, instilling in the community a greater sense of confidence in our schools.

THE INCLUSIVE GOAL-SETTING PROCESS

Many superintendents are familiar with the process of creating specific, measurable goals, but not all school leaders look for the opportunity to strengthen and build superintendent–school board relationships as they do this work. Inclusive goal setting is a four-step process you can use to work more effectively with your school board to change your schools for the better in a sustainable and thoughtful way. The elements of an inclusive goal-setting process include (1) frontloading; (2) identifying possible goals; (3) drafting goals; and (4) communicating progress toward goal attainment.[1] An inclusive goal-setting process begins with frontloading to prepare school board members for important areas of focus. This step requires you to create a thoughtful, honest, and sincere goal reflection, showing opportunities for improvement in your district. The next step in the process is identifying possible goals, reflecting both your interests and the school board's interests, which is followed by drafting the actual goals. Your ongoing communication of progress toward goal attainment, emphasizing the collective accomplishments of your team, is a final step and another important part of this process, helping build the school board's trust and confidence in you.

Step 1: Frontloading

Frontloading is a way for you to use goal reflections to prepare your school board to endorse what I call "high-impact" goals or reform-minded goals that can lead to significant improvements for students. Earlier in this chapter, you read about a school board that demanded results in their high performing district. Not all school boards approach the work in this same thoughtful manner; some simply "rubber stamp" the goals submitted by the superintendent, losing an important opportunity to weigh in on the kind of dialogue and debate that leads to better outcomes for students. If your school board takes little interest in your district goals, you are apt to give this task less of your time and attention, and the quality of your work may suffer. While the work is undeniably easier if school boards are less concerned with how you spend your days, most superintendents will say that their students deserve more. You have an obligation to identify challenging goals that will be of greatest benefit to your students, and your school board may need your expertise and guidance to help them set higher expectations for the district.

Frontloading is a strategy you can use to create a new level of awareness about district issues, preparing your school board for goals that you believe will have the greatest impact on your students. An effective way to frontload is to begin with your honest reflection about a high-impact goal, explaining a problem in the district, why it is a problem, and how students will benefit if there is a change. I used the goal-reflection process to begin publicly discussing my concerns (and the concerns of some school board members) about the increase in the number of students who were dropping out of school. This document defines the problems and challenges that must be confronted and lays the groundwork for improvement. I also incorporate reflection in my self-evaluations and superintendent reports, and I use this information to help shape my goals and action steps, further strengthening superintendent–school board relationships.

Frontloading can be a challenge if you experience tension between what the school board hopes to accomplish and what you believe to be in the best interests of students. If the reflection and your art of persuasion are not enough to influence the school board, then you may have more work to do. Your priorities may include addressing certain issues such as putting the most qualified teachers with those students who have the greatest need or ensuring that all elementary students are reading on level by grade three. School board members are elected officials, so they may have different ideas about what matters most. For instance, they may want to allocate resources to address current community concerns, such as handling transportation challenges or expanding extracurricular opportunities for elementary and middle school students. When appropriate, a good way to overcome this incompatibility of goals is to address some of these school board needs while also tackling the larger issues facing the schools. For example, addressing extracurricular activities for middle school students can be something you can begin to address without necessarily making it a district goal. Frontloading the challenges helps define the problem area you wish to address and establishes a shared understanding about the issue, increasing the likelihood that the school board will buy into your preferences and lend their full support to this important district goal.

Reflection is an often-overlooked step in the goal-setting process, but to my mind it is the most useful because it helps you focus on what matters most and the new steps you can take to make improvements in your schools. Superintendents work in an era of accountability, so you have a tendency to focus on problem solving and action steps, perhaps at times forgetting to build a solid basis of understanding. Reflection is an important first step in the inclusive goal-setting process, giving you an opportunity to name a problem or issue in the district and explain why it is necessary to dedicate your time, energy, talents, and resources to this particular challenge.

In my view, it is your responsibility as superintendent to identify problems and name issues in the school system that get in the way of student success, but coming to consensus on high-impact goals can be challenging. Naming the problem goes a long way, and even in highly contentious relationships between superintendents and school boards, there is typically some respect for your position, so often school boards can be persuaded when you make the effort to define and take responsibility for a problem. Addressing the student dropout rate, for example, can be a sensitive subject that people may not want to discuss. Feelings of helplessness can come in to play, and members of your team may find themselves asking questions like: How do I help students who do not want to be here? What about students who are without a home and have no support system? If a student has shown up for only one day of school in the last six months, what can I do to change his mind? To successfully combat the dropout rate, I knew I needed the pressure and support of the school board to help shift these mindsets, and goal reflection was my way of inviting school board members to take the lead.

The goal reflection in exhibit 5.1 provides context for the goal and includes an analysis of the issue. Developing an honest and thoughtful background for the goal you are proposing, identifying the problem, demonstrating to the school community an understanding of the challenges involved, and showing the school board that you care are all important in the frontloading process. A helpful context provides data and information to assist in the development of a goal that is meaningful, measurable, attainable, and focused on improving student outcomes. As shown in this example, you may also wish to reference current research and best practices related to the issue, as these data may lead to the development of action steps that are more meaningful. Finally, it is helpful for you to reference any strategies or actions currently underway that may relate to the topic, increasing the likelihood of goal attainment.

Step 2: Identifying Possible Goals

The next step is to map out possible goals from your perspective and that of the school board, starting with your strategic priorities. In chapter 4, I shared four strategic priorities that were developed through the strategic planning process (1) Post-Secondary Pursuits—We will work continuously to improve student achievement and prepare all learners for successful post-secondary pursuits; (2) Personalization—We will create safe, inclusive, and personalized learning environments for all students; (3) Communication—We will develop clear and effective forms of communication to enhance teaching and learning; and (4) Resources—We will maximize our resources of time, talent, and finances. As you consider possible district goals that are worthy of your time and attention, you should begin with your district's strategic priorities.

You can begin to identify goals by gathering documents such as the entry plan, the norms and beliefs, the strategic plan, and copies of your most recent evaluations and goals, which may spark new ideas and generate possibilities. In addition to reviewing these documents, I make it a point to reflect on the unique needs and desires of my school board members, creating a list like the

EXHIBIT 5.1 Goal reflection

GOAL REFLECTION:

The average dropout rate for the school system between 2006 and 2010 was 4.4% until a recent uptick in the number of students dropping out of school. Although a 5.3% dropout rate is significantly lower than what it was in the past, it goes without saying that even one student dropping out of school is too many, and further analysis of the problem is warranted. It appears that dropout rates in the city are higher for tenth graders, for males, and for Hispanic students, which aligns with trends seen in other urban communities and in the research.

Interesting facts and figures that we can draw upon to address this goal include:

1. Only about 58% of Hispanic students and 53% of black students will graduate on time with a regular diploma compared to 80% of Asian students and 76% of white students (Educational Projects in Education, 2007).
2. Graduation rates are significantly lower in districts with higher percentages of students who are eligible for free or reduced-price lunches—a measure of poverty (Swanson, 2004).
3. In 2006, the U.S. Bureau of the Census noted average income by educational attainment: High School Dropout—$17,299; High School Diploma —$26,933; Associate's Degree—$36,645; Bachelor's Degree—$52,671.
4. The lowest achieving 25% of students are twenty times more likely to drop out of high school than the highest achievement quartile (Carnevale, 2001).
5. Each dropout over the course of his/her lifetime costs the nation approximately $260,000 (Rouse, 2005).

Two years ago, we established a virtual learning program to help keep our students in school, and the high school administrators and I worked together on an initial dropout prevention plan. This goal is a continuation of our work on this issue, and we believe that the establishment of an alternative high school will help us keep our students in school. We know that the traditional day school does not meet the needs of every student, and it is our hope that a better understanding of the students at risk of dropping out of school, as well as an increase in opportunities for learning in alternative settings, will reduce, if not prevent, the likelihood that one of our students becomes a statistic.

Dropout Rates Over Time

2004–2005	2005–2006	2006–2007	2007–2008	2008–2009	2009–2010	2010–2011
6.8%	5.9%	4.7%	4.2%	4.3%	4.7%	5.3%

EXHIBIT 5.2 Goal possibilities list

Goal Possibilities

1. Enhance the work of PLCs (Julie)
2. Reduce the dropout rate by half (Julie/SC)
3. Establish a district assessment team (SC)
4. Standardize homework practices (SC)
5. Elementary foreign language (Julie/SC)
6. Increase number of awards/recognition (SC)
7. Capital needs/infrastructure (SC)
8. Sub plan for support services, including ABA, OT/PT (SC)
9. Inclusion (Julie)
10. State initiatives (SC)
11. Improvements in Mathematics (Julie/SC)
12. Increase participation in 2 and 4 year colleges, and Tier I schools (Julie)

one shown in exhibit 5.2. If you have taken the time to get to know your school board through the processes identified in the previous chapters (entry interviews, norms and beliefs, and strategic planning), identifying issues of greatest import for the school community and your school board members should be relatively easy for you. Identifying a school board member's interests is also an effective relationship-building strategy because board members have valuable insights to share, and they appreciate a school leader who takes the time to listen.

While it is impossible for you to effectively address every school board member's interest or concern, brainstorming a list of possible goals is a good way for you to let your school board know that you are open to their ideas. For instance, I included capital improvements and infrastructure on the list of proposed goals because this is of particular interest to some school board members. As it turned out, this recommended goal got traction with the majority of school board members, and it was adopted as a district goal. As you consider the needs and interests of your school board members, you may find that one is interested in the expansion of elementary foreign languages, one wants to improve mathematics performance at all levels, and another wants to create a special education backup plan to ensure therapies and supports are in place with no disruption in services. All these ideas have merit and are worthy of goal setting, and the most effective way to build relationships and get results is by getting consensus on goals that matter most to you, the school board, and your students.

Developing an agenda with the school board chair can be an effective method for structuring meetings to gain consensus on district goals. An example of an agenda for a workshop scheduled at the beginning of the school year to revise norms and beliefs and establish district goals is included in appendix 5.1. This should be posted as a public meeting and held off-site during a retreat if possible. While the work can be done during a school board meeting, it is important to keep in mind that this inclusive goal-setting process is designed to build relationships, so maximum school board participation is desired. School board members need to be able to ask many questions and engage in thoughtful dialogue throughout this process, and this approach is not in keeping with the business-like nature of a traditional school board meeting. At this meeting, you can share your list of possible district goals, obtaining input from school board members.

During the meeting, begin by talking about the process you used to develop the list, taking care to include the ways in which you have incorporated the school board's interests. Next, describe each item on your goal possibilities list, explaining why the item was important enough to include on the goal possibilities list, pointing out items that may have been left off the list and why.

For example, there might be an interest in expanding the number of field trips for students in each grade level, but that topic might be easily addressed with one declaration by the superintendent and may not require the ongoing focus and attention that would make it a district goal. District goals typically involve significant challenges, and they become more meaningful to the school board when you share your thinking about the importance of each one. For example, you may talk about one school board member's strong desire to expand science and technology in the elementary schools, how this is reflected in the strategic plan, and your reasons for believing that doing so will positively impact the students in your school system. You can then ask members to help you prioritize their preferred goals, asking them to rate the top three goal possibilities that they hope to see addressed in the district goals in the next year or two.

After the items are discussed and school board members have an opportunity to ask many questions, you can then ask them to take a few minutes on their own to identify their top three choices in order of preference. Next, read your list of goal priorities aloud, allowing school board members to determine their preferences together. This rating process is done most effectively when the school board first reflects on the recommended goals individually and then together as a group. You or the school board chair can tally by writing the initials of each board member next to the goal possibility that is on a list. When the tally is complete, you can encourage the school board members to further discuss and debate any goal possibility that they do not wish to make a district focus.

Dialogue and debate are always important, but they are especially so at this time because school board members' priorities tend to shift as a result of the group discussion, enabling the members to reach agreement about the district goals in a natural, organic way. You may also find the conversation helpful because you will quickly develop an understanding of what areas of concern are most important to the school board and why. Once the school board selects the top three goal possibilities from the list, you can check in again with the board to reaffirm the school board's interests, or you can request a more formal approach, recommending a motion for you to pursue the three goal areas of interest as identified by the school board. In either case, the minutes of the meeting should reflect the school board's preferences for the three district goals that they want you to address in the upcoming school year.

Step 3: Drafting Goals

Now, imagine that the school board has identified these three goal areas of focus from your goal possibilities list: (1) make significant improvements in mathematics, (2) reduce the dropout rate by half, and (3) address capital needs and infrastructure. How can you take these goal preferences and turn them into meaningful written goals that will advance the work of the school system and help students? Dialogue is a good way to begin, and the school board's conversation about the prioritization of goals gives you a window into their thought process, and it helps to shape the development of a goal, the action steps, and your evidence or indicators of success. The school board members reflect the attitudes and beliefs of a school community, and by listening closely and carefully, you begin to develop an understanding and appreciation for how they view their challenges and opportunities for growth. You should reflect on the conversation with your school board around a particular topic for a district goal, and begin to draft these goals by writing a thoughtful reflection to contextualize the issue. If your school board adopted your high-impact goal or goals, your reflection work will already be done. The school board may have decided to add district goals that you were not anticipating, in which case your goal reflection will not be complete. If the school board wants you to create a district goal around a topic that you had not anticipated, the goal reflection becomes even more important, as it provides you with an opportunity to clarify your own thoughts about how to tackle a specific goal.

After you have developed the reflection for a particular district goal, it becomes easier to write the goal itself, along with the action steps and indicators of success. In a 1981 issue of *Management Review,* George Doran was the first to use the mnemonic device "SMART goals," a popular approach to writing goals that are specific, measurable, attainable, realistic, and timely.[2] As schools have entered an era of greater accountability over the past decade, more attention has been given to the development of goals that are measurable. The way in which goals are structured may vary, but no matter what process you choose to create a goal, it is important for you to identify clearly what it is you hope to do, define the time frame for accomplishing the goal, and explain how you intend to measure the progress. In addition, careful consideration should be given to the alignment of the school system's strategic plan. Adherence to a vision, a mission, and the strategic priorities of a school system brings much-needed stability and coherence fundamental to the success of any school system; if the goal area you are addressing does not align with those elements of your strategic plan, you and your school board need to rethink how best to focus your efforts.

When you are developing action items and indicators of success, you should consider the involvement of school board members. School board members want to contribute and be part of the progress being made in a school system, and when you can find ways to engage them in meaningful work, you build effective relationships with your school board members. In an inclusive goal-setting process, school board members oversee and approve your goals, which provides them with an authentic opportunity to contribute to the school community. In the action steps that follow, you also identify multiple actions that lend themselves to the involvement of school board members.

Indicators of success like those seen in exhibit 5.3 correspond with each action item and serve as evidence of your progress toward goal attainment. They also represent a way for school board members to interact with you and monitor progress. School board members can and should request evidence of your progress throughout the year. As evaluators, they may want to see the tracking system, the meeting notes with the principal, or a flyer announcing the grand opening of the "early college" high school, and they should have that option. School board members also appreciate cost estimates and funding information, and they are likely to request this information, so it is helpful to identify up front the monetary impacts in the district goals. Including this information in the goals eliminates surprises, provides you with another layer of approval beyond the budgeting process, and represents one more way for you to build trust with your school board. It is further recommended that you request formal school

EXHIBIT 5.3 Evidence/indicators of success

EVIDENCE/INDICATORS OF SUCCESS:

2.1 Dropout prevention goal shared with all high school administrators, who write their own dropout prevention goal (September, 2012). Memos, newsletters, and school board reports and presentations to highlight the dropout problem and the actions we intend to take to address it.

2.2 Individual meeting notes with the principal to support and monitor high school progress.

2.3 An analysis of the lowest achieving 25% of students and a tracking system to identify who is most at risk and the actions that we are taking or will take to better address their needs.

2.4 Identification of additional funding sources to support the alternative high school.

2.5 Grand opening event in January, 2013.

2.6 Alternative high school job descriptions and staffing reports with official appointments.

2.7 A creative and innovative "early college" alternative high school curriculum that emphasizes personalization, self-exploration and awareness, collaboration, and post-secondary pursuits.

2.8 School board presentation and minutes.

Funding:

Action 2.5 Alternative high school start-up costs estimated at $500,000.

Action 2.6 Alternative high school director/principal estimated at $90,000.

Action 2.7 Development of the alternative high school curricula estimated at $20,000.

board approval of your goals, ensuring that when it comes time for your evaluation there is clarity in the work that is expected of you.

Action items and timelines are another important feature in the goal-setting process. Exhibit 5.4 shows the key actions and timelines developed to accomplish goal 2 of the strategic plan to reduce the dropout rate by half. School board members frequently offer insightful ideas for actions that can help achieve a goal. For example, school board members might request a more targeted and

EXHIBIT 5.4 Key actions/timelines

KEY ACTIONS/TIMELINES:

2.1 Continue to create awareness of the problem; share data with the public and with administrators particular to those populations at risk, such as tenth grade students who are male and Hispanic (October, 2012).

2.2 Include in individual meetings with the high school principal, a periodic review of the High School Dropout Prevention Plan (October, December, February, and May).

2.3 Broaden the scope of responsibility to better address the needs of students at risk of dropping out of school, and establish a system for tracking preventative measures taken. For example, guidance counselors, administrators, and curriculum supervisors may submit rosters of students whom they deem to be at risk of dropping out and any actions taken, such as phone logs, home visits, or referrals (October, 2012).

2.4 Pursue grant funds to maximize resources and create unique learning opportunities for our students at risk of dropping out (2012–2013).

2.5 Work with the "Early College" Alternative High School Task Force to create an optimal alternative educational setting in the city (January, 2012–May, 2013).

2.6 Develop a job description and hire a talented director/leader to run the alternative high school; in addition, hire talented, dedicated staff, including the necessary support staff to address the social and emotional needs of our students, ensuring success (August–December, 2012).

2.7 Develop innovative educational practices and curricula that provide creative, experienced and career-based opportunities to learn (November–January, 2012).

2.8 Invite administration to school board meeting to discuss progress on this goal (February, 2013).

strategic approach to monitoring students at risk, recommending personal phone calls home. As previously suggested, you are encouraged to include updates on monthly superintendent's reports concerning your progress toward goal attainment.

Step 4: Communicating Progress toward Goal Attainment

I include ongoing updates on my school system's progress toward achieving goals in biweekly superintendent reports. These written reports are shared during televised school board meetings and with the staff. Providing updates in newsletters is a helpful way to inform the community of your priorities and progress, as is making appearances on local talk shows or radio stations. As exhibit 5.5 illustrates, it can be useful to prepare a mid-year review related to the superintendent–school board goals to "reduce the dropout rate by half." The school board members can see your progress at a glance and provide feedback on your progress toward goal attainment. Keeping the school community apprised of the most important work happening in your school system is also important; the mid-cycle review presents an opportunity to share with the school board and community the district's progress toward completing the goals and the action items.

As we have seen in previous chapters, school reformers who are quick to change but slow to make relationships a priority are often eager to take credit for accomplishments. School board members need to have a sense of accomplishment too, and achievements should not be limited to yours as superintendent. As much as a superintendent might like to think that he is the sole catalyst for change, whether it is a result of policy or financial approvals, it is unlikely for changes in any school system to occur without the support of the school board, so why not give them the credit they deserve? My school board played an important role in the creation of a new "early college" alternative high school for students who were at risk of dropping out of school. As you will see in chapter 8, I recognized them publicly for their efforts, helping to strengthen our relationship. The school board took great pride in knowing that they had a hand in helping more students graduate and go on to college. "Positive begets positive," and when you include goal achievement updates in newsletters, or you discuss the district's progress during speaking engagements in the business community, it can go a long way to give credit to the school board and all who have helped make the achievements possible. School boards and school communities matter,

EXHIBIT 5.5 Superintendent's mid-year review

SUPERINTENDENT'S MID-YEAR REVIEW

Indicator	Description	Timeline/Budget	Status/Notes
2.1—Dropout Awareness	Continue to create awareness of the problem; share data with the public and with administrators particular to those populations at risk (e.g., males, Hispanic, Grade 10).	October, 2012. N/A	In Progress • Supt Reports • Admin Dropout Presentation on Jan. 17, 2013
2.2—Review Admin Dropout Efforts	Include a periodic review of the High School Dropout Prevention Plan in individual meetings with the high school principal.	October, December, February, May N/A	In Progress • Mid-Yr Review • Check-In with curr. sups.
2.3—Preventative Dropout Measures	Broaden the scope of responsibility to better address the needs of students at risk of dropping out of school, and establish a system for tracking preventative measures taken. For example, guidance counselors, administrators and curriculum supervisors may submit rosters of students at risk.	October, 2012 N/A	In Progress • See Dropout Goals submitted by all admin.
2.4—Grants for At-Risk Youth	Pursue grant funds to maximize resources and create unique learning opportunities for our students at risk of dropping out (2012–2013).	2012–2013 N/A	Ongoing • 21st Century Grant - $168,000 • Counseling Grant - $30,000
2.5—"Early College" AHS Task Force	Work with the Alternative High School Task Force to create a post-secondary partnership, and in an optimal educational setting in the city.	2012–2013 $500,000	Ongoing • Task Force Min. • AHS Plan
2.6—AHS Leadership	Develop a job description and hire a talented director/leader to run the alternative high school; in addition, hire talented, dedicated staff, including the necessary support staff to address the social and emotional needs of our students, ensuring success.	August–Dec., 2012 $90,000	Ongoing • Job Description • Consultant hired • Staffing Postings • Re-advertise principal/dir.
2.7—Career-Based and Innovative Curricula	Develop innovative educational practices and curricula that provide creative, experienced, and career-based opportunities to learn.	Nov.–Jan., 2012 $20,000	Ongoing • AHS Plan • Job Entrepreneur position
2.8—Dropout Efforts	Invite high school administration to discuss progress on this goal at board meeting.	February, 2013 N/A	In Progress • See SC Planner

and if you are an effective superintendent, you know that you are able to accomplish only a fraction of what is possible for your students without the support of your school board and many others.

Good leaders have a vision, and exceptional leaders are able to work with their school boards to develop concrete goals to make that collective vision become a reality. It is the responsibility of both you and your school board members to work together to create challenging goals that will improve teaching and learning, creating better opportunities for the students you serve. These inclusive goals should be respectful of the school culture and unique to your community, with the power to transform the lives of children. Inclusive goal setting works, and there is no better way to build a winning, productive team than by meeting and exceeding the challenges that you and your school board set for yourselves on behalf of your students.

APPENDIX 5.1 Agenda for Strategic Priorities

AGENDA

School Committee Workshop
October 10, 2012
4:00–8:30 p.m.

Purpose
High functioning school systems evolve when dedicated educational leaders understand that students are the primary focus. In an effort to lead by example, the Taunton School Committee made a formal commitment in 2009 to conduct biannual workshops designed to give the Superintendent and the School Committee an opportunity to focus on how we work together and how we can improve. This is the first of two workshops we will have this year to review and reflect upon our "norms and beliefs."

Pre-Work
All participants are asked to carefully review the Taunton Norms and Beliefs, and complete the self-assessment. Data will be collected and compiled in advance of the workshop. You are asked to share your self-assessment with the Superintendent and/or the School Committee Chairperson by no later than Tuesday, October 9, 2012.

Anticipated Outcomes:
1. Reflect upon our individual and group progress to date;
2. Revise and reaffirm the "TPS Norms and Beliefs";
3. Develop consensus on strategic priorities to inform goals.

Time	Item(s)
4:00–4:30 p.m.	Opening
4:45–5:00 p.m.	Review Purpose, Agenda, and Outcomes
5:00–6:00 p.m.	Norms and Beliefs Activity—review the self-assessment data to determine areas of strength and opportunities for improvement for each one of the three categories: • How We Govern (20 minutes) • How We Communicate (20 minutes) • How We Improve (20 minutes)
6:00–7:00 p.m.	Working Dinner • School Committee Meeting Planner: 2012–2013
7:00–8:15 p.m.	Consensus on Strategic Priorities for Goal-Setting • Professional Learning Communities • Reduce the dropout rate by half by 2014 • Establish a District Assessment Team • Improve teaching and learning • Elementary foreign language • Recognition and Outreach • MCAS School-Improvement • Capital Needs/Infrastructure • Special Education Achievement • Inclusion • State and Local Initiatives • Streamline Personnel and Student Services • Mathematics Achievement • Post-Secondary Pursuits • Implement goal-setting processes
8:15–8:30 p.m.	Reflections—participants will have an opportunity to reflect upon the conversation, and share personal insights by responding to the following: *"As a result of our work together this evening, I have more clarity on . . ."*

CHAPTER SIX

On Matters of Race, Class, Power, and Culture: Leading Together

The ultimate measure of a [leader] is not where he stands in moments of comfort and convenience, but where he stands at times of challenge and controversy.

—MARTIN LUTHER KING, JR.

EDUCATIONAL REFORM often means introducing systemic changes that touch on issues of race, class, power, and culture. Because of increasingly diverse populations and the segregated nature of U.S. housing, many systemic reforms utilized today like closing and consolidating neighborhood schools, reallocating monies to new programs, or changing and moving staff are likely to provoke strong opinions in the community about the desirability of change and calculations about who benefits (and who does not). How these reforms are formulated and communicated and—most critically—implemented can make all the difference in their sustainability and success. Changing the status quo does not mean that a community has to be disregarded, disrespected, or devalued; rather, bold changes can be an opportunity to collaborate, forge stronger connections, and help a community coalesce around ideas that will make a difference in the lives of children.

> ### COMMUNITY INPUT TEAM PROCESS
>
> **MATERIALS NEEDED**
>
> - Strategic plan
> - Norms and protocols
> - List of issues
>
> **THE PROCESS**
>
> 1. Reflect on your challenge and define the problem.
> 2. Establish a district transition team.
> 3. Create a web of opportunity.
> 4. Enlist administrators and assign charges.
> 5. Bring your blockers to the table.
> 6. Face the public.
> 7. Develop a communication plan.

School reform can give superintendents an opportunity to lead with their school board and school community, making significant changes as they simultaneously strengthen their relationships. An effective way to implement systemic reform is by utilizing a process that I developed called the *community input team (CIT) process*. The community input team process is a powerful model for change that puts the community at the center of the reform movement, by including them in the implementation of a major initiative.

Chances are good that as a leader of your district you have established goals and strategic plans designed to improve outcomes for all students. Ambitious school reforms that include social justice aims can be the most challenging because they call into question the hearts, minds, and intentions of others. Even the most fearless, experienced leader may feel intimidated by these leadership challenges, causing some to avoid these contentious reforms altogether. The more bold and courageous school reformers may run headlong into the effort, paying little attention to the concomitant risks that arise when implementation is shoddy. As mentioned earlier, a failed reform is worse than no reform at all, and these leaders may inflict more damage than they would have if they had never attempted to make changes in the first place. Superintendents can use the community input team process to their advantage, teaching others to strengthen their relationships as they confront the most pressing educational obstacles of our time.

THE MOST CHALLENGING REFORMS: RACE, POWER, CLASS, AND CULTURE

What makes matters of race, class, power, and culture so difficult for superintendents, school boards and school community members? As a rule, human beings are resistant to change, and maintaining the status quo gives them a sense of security. If changes are foisted upon them, it is human nature to sit back like a sage with arms crossed, waiting knowingly for the disastrous result that was predicted. Superintendents are faced with significant challenges every day, but those who thrive understand that strong leadership is needed to address the urgent needs of your students, and this hinges on your ability to embrace these challenges. Leaders who steer clear of solving pressing problems that could negatively impact the public's perception of them are not really leaders at all. If you shy away from these challenges, you lose sight of the meaningful reforms that your students need you to champion, and you miss an opportunity to build strong, lasting relationships with your school board.

When you lead school reform efforts, you may be asking the school board and school community members to change everything they know about education, and in so doing, you are often asking these community members to confront their own beliefs and attitudes about race and privilege. This chapter illustrates how I used the community input team process to close and consolidate schools; it also describes the community response to the integration of poor students and those of color into a middle school in an upper middle class, predominantly white neighborhood.

A SCHOOL REFORM CHALLENGE

My school board had just voted to move forward with a school closure and consolidation plan when it became clear to me that the school reform effort we were about to tackle had even higher stakes than I once thought. I remember the day well; after many hectic late-night meetings, my husband, two boys, and I decided to drive to the mountains of New Hampshire for one perfect, peaceful night of rest and relaxation. We were enjoying our time at an outdoor café when I heard the familiar buzz of my Blackberry. Without thinking, I glanced down to check my messages, a habit that irritated my youngest son, whose usual response came right on cue, "Mom, put that thing away."

It turns out I should have listened to him that day because the scathing e-mail I received bothered me terribly. It was from an angry parent demanding to know if it was true that students from a certain school in our district would now be included at his child's school. He told me to take him seriously because he was a reputable businessman who made a significant six-figure salary, and he moved his family to the current school to get away from "those kids." I wrote him back immediately to let him know that, yes, we were planning to consolidate schools, the school board had taken their vote, and I was sorry that he was so upset about the decision. I promised that we would do our best to ensure that the transition would be smooth for everyone, including his child. I also expressed optimism that more diversity in our schools and the additional resources that would come from the closures and consolidations would make a positive difference for all the children in our city. No sooner had I hit Send on my e-mail message when I received this reply: "I wouldn't send my golden retriever to one of your schools." I was floored because I had never experienced that level of overt disdain, and I learned that day that it is something that all school leaders must be prepared for and willing to confront.

The massive school reform we were undertaking was high stakes. As I thought about ways to successfully tackle this challenge, many questions went through my mind. Can this school consolidation and closure even be done, and if so, can I manage to keep my relationships with the school board and school community intact? What leadership skills, techniques, and strategies can be used to ease the worries of a concerned public? Who needs the most support as we make these changes? How do I work with my school board to gain their confidence and help prepare them for the outcry they are sure to hear from large segments of the school community? Will I have the courage to press on if people get cold feet and no one else but me wants to tackle these school reforms?

Many urban school superintendents experience fairly significant leadership challenges on a regular basis, and I am no exception. There have been reductions in force, staff dismissals, public relations nightmares, and worst of all, tragedies in our school community. One of the greatest challenges of my career, however, involved this school consolidation and closure reform effort that shook our community for a time. I had just been appointed superintendent, and we needed to address a significant structural deficit and issues of equity in our schools. While personnel and public relations issues were commonplace, solving problems of this magnitude was unchartered territory for me. A brand new superintendent in this school system, I took pride in thumbing my nose at those contemporary school reformers with their disregard for the school community and their "take no prisoners" approach to change, and I assumed my genuine care and concern would help ease the burden of these transitions. While the school system's problems might have been obvious to me, the pathway to resolution was not.

I began to dig in to the problem, and together with the school board, we commissioned two studies: a demographics study and a capacity utilization study. After we examined the data, it became clear that some schools were out of compliance with the Americans with Disabilities Act (ADA) and desperately in need of repair with no funding to resolve these issues. In addition, there were approximately one thousand four hundred empty seats in the newly renovated $112 million high school. The other issue that reared its ugly head was the lack of equity in the four middle schools, and the school serving our poorest and most diverse population in the city was the only one lacking extra- and co-curricular activities, quality science labs, a theater, a stage, and performing arts.

Initially, as we discussed ways to tackle these challenges, short-term solutions seemed preferable to most school board members. School closures had not happened in the past, and maintaining the status quo was a safer bet; a few were ready to tackle the challenge head-on, whereas others reasoned that we should close only one school and wait to resolve the other problems at a future date and time. I worried that a slow and steady distribution of pain year after year would take its toll on the climate and culture in our schools, compromising our students, staff, and my ability to lead effectively. I therefore wanted to take care of the challenges in one fell swoop. Sensing reluctance and trepidation, I brought the school board back to our norms and beliefs protocol that we had developed together. We discussed one of those norms and beliefs in detail: "The Superintendent intends to seek comprehensive solutions to problems and will create clear structures for decision making. In the spirit of continuous improvement, these structures may be revisited at any time." I reasoned that it was not healthy for students or staff if we decided to bite off a chunk of the problem at a time. I then began to find ways to prepare the school board and community for these changes. I asked the school board to vote on a decision-making timeline that I developed, as seen in exhibit 6.1, signaling to the school community that this was not idle chatter about closures, and one way or another, a decision would be made.

After many meetings, many conversations, and several attempts by school board members and others to develop alternate creative proposals to help us deal with our structural deficit and inequities, a solid solution began to emerge. I let the school board know that my recommendation would be to simultaneously redistrict, close three elementary schools, implement a reduction in force, repurpose a middle school, and move the entire eighth grade into the high school—and I wanted to do this simultaneously. An administrator who was not one to speak out on any issue took me aside to be sure I understood the enormity of the undertaking and to let me know that in his recollection there had never been a single school closure in the city's history, never mind three, along with redistricting and consolidations. Another school board member who was friendly with many educators in the system also let me know that some had the feeling that this was "way too much and way too soon," and I should look for alternative solutions to the problem. I greatly respected both of these individuals and knew they were trying to be helpful. To be honest, their concern made me a bit weak in the knees, but I was in this for the long haul, and I felt certain that the time to do this was now—and all at once—to prevent prolonged turmoil for our school community. I let myself trust my instincts, and I put my faith in the school community and in our superintendent–school board team.

And so began the painful process of educational reform in one urban school community. The school closure and consolidation options were presented

EXHIBIT 6.1 Decision-making timeline

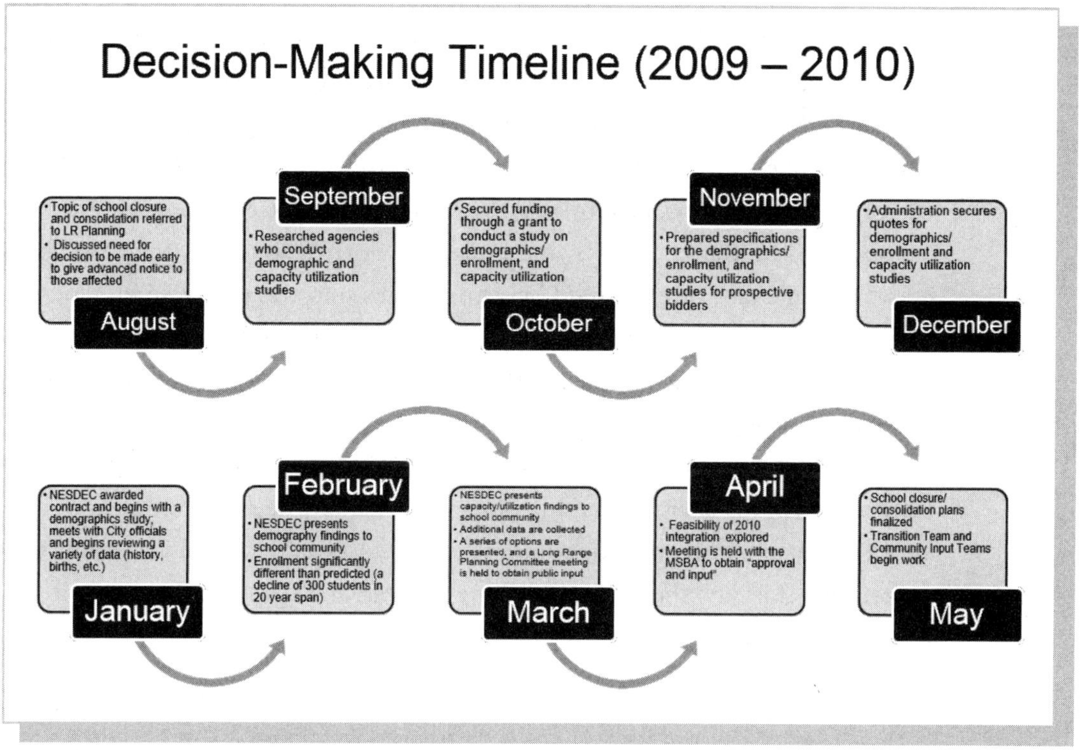

publicly, and I worked with the school board to hold community forums. Community members reacted in ways that they had every right to: they were indignant and outraged, and students spoke out publicly about their fears and the negative effect these transitions would have on their lives. The unions were not happy, and former school leaders and city officials publicly lambasted the school board and me for devising such an absurd plan. This public outcry took its toll on school board members, and their feelings vacillated from confidence ("this is the right thing to do for kids") to uncertainty ("but do we really need to do this all right now?"). I spent much of my time reassuring the board, patiently answering any and all of their questions, and preparing them for the challenges ahead. On the night the vote was taken, students, parents, community members, city officials, and current and former educators came out in droves. The public spoke out in fierce opposition, the scene was somewhat chaotic, and the school board chair had to call well-respected individuals out of order. Somehow we survived.

Once the school board vote was finally taken (seven in favor and one in opposition), I was exhausted, but the real work had only just begun. In the preceding months I had listened to the public foreshadow the inevitable problems with our school closure and consolidation plan, and I listened to the countless testimonials by concerned educators, parents, and students. I worried about the impact of failed school reforms on students, and I knew my leadership was on the line. A lot was riding on my ability to see these sweeping changes through, and establish positive relationships in the process. I asked myself what it would take for someone to convert me or persuade me that something I was dead-set against was actually worthwhile. My answer was that I would have to be a part of the change process with some serious decision-making power. Ultimately, I devised a plan to create a community input team process designed to involve the school community in the reform effort and the decision-making process, and I presented my plan to the school board and to the public.

COMMUNITY INPUT TEAMS: A WAY TO REFORM AND RELATE

The problem with school reform today is that some leaders focus exclusively on the reform itself, and not on its effective implementation. Educational pioneers say that transformation from the ground up is needed in our schools, but reformers in the United States should pay more attention to the implementation of these ideas because Americans are notorious for instituting big changes without a carefully constructed implementation plan. Those on both sides of the aisle likely agree that the passage of the Affordable Care Act (ACA) is a case in point; the President of the United States passed sweeping health-care reforms with the goal of lowering insurance costs for all, but the failed launch of the federal marketplace made it difficult for Americans to enroll. Implementation matters.

When the implementation of a reform is not a priority for the leader, skeptics grow increasingly more critical, and supporters begin to doubt. Educational reformers intent on making their mark focus on getting a reform passed, but in many cases the work is only just beginning and an equivalent amount of effort that went into getting the reform passed should be expended on the plan to implement the changes. The *community input team process* is an inclusive relationship-building strategy that I developed to help you effectively implement reform and strengthen ties with your school community. The seven steps associated with the community input team process are (1) reflect on your challenge and define the problem; (2) establish a district transition team; (3) create a web of opportunity; (4) enlist administrators and assign charges; (5) bring your blockers to the table; (6) face the public; and (7) develop a communication plan.

Step 1: Reflect on Your Challenge and Define the Problem

After we made the decision to comprehensively tackle reforms in the district, we immediately turned our attention to the effective implementation of these reforms. Closing just one school was a massive undertaking, never mind closing three, redistricting, and consolidating schools all at once. It was apparent that a thoughtful, organized approach was necessary, so I began by defining the problem as an issue of equity and finance, and I began to talk about this at school board meetings and community forums. I then brainstormed a list of action steps to ensure a smooth transition, and these would later become the charges of the community input teams.

Step 2: Establish a District Transition Team

I knew that for the school reforms to be successful, the school board and school community had to take ownership and an active role in the implementation of the changes. I developed an oversight team that I called the district transition team (or DTT) composed of school board members, administrators, and community members. The DTT was effective because I, as superintendent, was also a part of the team, and we utilized a distributive or shared model of leadership. Community input teams, chosen by myself and my administrators, were smaller groups with eight to ten school community members assigned specific tasks. The CITs reported directly to the DTT that acted as a sounding board for them, having the final say on decisions that were proposed. If we were unable to make decisions together and come to consensus in the group, I reserved the right as superintendent of schools to make the final call.

Step 3: Create a Web of Opportunity

In the months leading up to the school closure and consolidation, the community expressed their concerns, and I took note of every issue. I knew that the school board members were facing the scrutiny of their friends, family, and neighbors, and I wanted to make certain that we addressed all concerns, we corrected any oversights, and we got the reforms right. After I had developed a list of all the issues, I then clustered the emergent themes in a web, demonstrating that a particular topic was significant enough to warrant its own community input team. Next, I developed an overarching district transition team and winnowed down the list of issues to be addressed by a total of nine community input teams, including (1) athletics, (2) grade eight transitions, (3) redistricting/transportation, (4) curriculum and professional development, (5) moving and logistics, (6) scheduling, (7) middle school transition and repurposing, (8) high school logistics and grade eight pilot, and (9) special education.

Step 4: Enlist Administrators and Assign Charges

Next, I appointed my administrators to lead a community input team, and I assigned the following team leadership responsibilities and guidelines:

- Membership will be varied and include those for and against school consolidation, students, parents, and a school board designee.
- Whenever possible, CIT leaders will begin with a thorough review of existing literature and other sources of data, including school community surveys/interviews, site visits, interviews with other educators, and so on.
- Plans must be submitted in writing and include a specific set of recommendations, clearly stating the pros and cons of each, to be considered by the district transition team.

- A communication plan must be part of the plan submitted to ensure that all stakeholders are aware of the recommendations being made.
- The CIT leader will be responsible for compiling agendas, minutes, and research; finding cost-efficient solutions; assembling groups; making plans that answer the given charge; meeting on a regular basis, implementing approved components, and accurately reporting to the DTT.

Then I gave specific instructions for the issues that needed to be resolved based on the concerns that I heard expressed by the community. For instance, I assigned the Grade 8 Transition Community Input Team three important tasks, asking them to (1) work closely with the Logistics CIT and school principals to develop a Grade 8 Transition Plan for the district and for all students who would be affected, including those in the three remaining middle schools; (2) explore topics of interest and areas of concern for students and parents (i.e., graduation, class trips, student council); and (3) organize eighth grade tours of the high school for students and parents from all four middle schools. Exhibit 6.2 illustrates the tasks or charges assigned to each CIT.

Even though the "golden retriever" e-mail from the angry parent was out of line, this parent's message still provided an important take-away for me: he was concerned about how the transition would affect his child, who would also be impacted by the changes in the sense that the school community that she knew would be drastically changed when new students became part of her school's culture. How many other parents and caregivers would feel this way about the changes and not be able to express their concern? My focus had been on the students who were *leaving* their school and the sense of loss they might experience when they had to abandon the school they loved. However troubling the remarks, this parent helped remind me that transitions work both ways, and as seen in the first task I assigned, I made sure to incorporate this concern into an area that we would later address. We had to consider the needs of the students who were *staying*, as well as those we were *sending* to new schools after their schools had closed.

EXHIBIT 6.2 CIT charges

#	Community Input Teams	Charge
1	Athletics	• Using existing resources, examine athletic opportunities, MIAA requirements, logistics (including the availability of space for practices/contests) for Grade 8 students moving to THS (Phase I - Gr 8 Accelerated Pilot and Phase II).
2	Curriculum/ Professional Development	• Inventory all schools to ensure that appropriate instructional materials exist to accommodate students in new buildings (Phase I). • Work with teachers to ensure that curriculum for Grade 8 students is engaging, developmentally appropriate, and teachers have the appropriate support and professional development (Phase II).
3	Mulcahey Transition	• Using materials provided by the Redistricting/Transportation Team, work with students and families to acclimate them to their new middle school (Phase I).
4	Gr 8 Transitions	• Work closely with Logistics CIT and school principals to develop a Gr 8 Transition CIT for the district and for all Gr 8 students who will be affected (Friedman, Martin, Parker). • Explore topics of interest for students and parents, including graduation, class trips, student council, etc. • Organize Grade 8 tours of THS for students and parents from all schools.

Step 5: Bring Your Blockers to the Table

Throughout my career in leadership, I have operated under the assumption that it is always better to invite those who may not agree with me on a given topic to be part of the conversation. First, whether I want to admit it or not, there is probably something I can learn from them. Second, although it can be frustrating, I have the greatest (and perhaps only) hope of turning around a sour relationship if I show that I am genuinely willing to work with them. In my more than two decades in education, I have learned that this approach almost always pays off in some way, so I incorporated it into my CIT model by instructing each of the nine CIT leaders to reach out to others who may be more outspoken on their topic. For example, we should invite to be a member of the Athletics CIT that person who had a lot to say at the community forums about how athletics would be ruined if eighth graders were consolidated at the high school level. I made it clear that the CITs needed to mirror the population at large, which meant the groups should reflect our diversity and include those who were for and against the school closures and consolidations.

As we discussed the importance of bringing naysayers or blockers to the table, I made certain to model this by putting one of my blockers on my district transition team. The whole purpose of the DTT and CIT process is to effectively implement changes and to build trust, allaying the fears and concerns of the community. When it comes to challenging reforms, one of the only ways to do this is to listen to those who might have opinions that we did not want to hear. My "blocker" was the parent of a seventh grader who was strongly opposed to putting her daughter in the high school at such an early age. She worried about the bad influence of the older children at the high school and about all the things her child and others would miss if they were unable to participate in the traditional activities that the rest of the eighth graders had in middle school. Her insights on the DTT helped us experience the school reforms from a different perspective, and our willingness to listen, respond, and correct our course helped change her views of our effort. When parents lashed out during the ensuing forums, she calmly shared that she experienced the same feelings and talked about how much the process and our willingness to listen had meant to her. This blocker ended up being one of the most helpful and persuasive members of the DTT, and she even participated in the community forums, advocating for the school closures and consolidations. Even though this parent was saddened that her daughter's education would be changing in ways she had not expected, she became one of our greatest allies in the school reform effort because she knew how much we cared.

Throughout the CIT process, I worked with my administrative team to clarify misinformation and publicly answer each and every question that was asked of us. I developed a series of "claims and facts" documents, like the one shown in exhibit 6.3, that I used in presentations, and school board members used as talking points with the public. We also had a process in place for gathering questions and answers, and we developed a document to share publicly. I asked all middle and high school principals to host a community forum in their buildings to bring their school community up to speed on the issues and gather all the questions they could. We then developed a question-and-answer list that we distributed to the public via e-mail blast, and we posted it on a Web site "transitions" link. I also discussed the questions and answers publicly at televised school board meetings. No question was too small to elicit an answer, and when a school board member, administrator, assistant, or custodian asked a question on behalf of a constituent, we found an answer as soon as possible and added it to our Q&A list. This approach was a good way for us to demonstrate that we we were not steamrolling the school reform with total disregard for the community, and it started to build the public's confidence and trust.

Step 6: Face the Public

Facing an angry mob is not easy, but when it comes to school reform, it must be done. With a well-structured agenda, a respectful mindset, and the ability to remain unflappable under pressure, withstanding vitriolic attacks from a grieving public not ready to embrace school reforms, you can circumvent larger issues that may arise. Righteous indignation comes in the form of marches in protest or votes of no confidence, especially if the public does not have its say; attempting to silence members of a school community and telling the media that you are "unavailable for comment" are common missteps made by overzealous school reformers. If you believe in what you are doing, you should be able to face the music, and the public should have the right to tell you exactly how they feel about it.

When I brought administrators together to let them know that we were going to host a forum for the parents and caregivers of all six hundred fifty rising eighth graders and any interested school community members, most warned me that it was a very bad idea. They reasoned that they had never seen the

EXHIBIT 6.3 CIT claim/facts sheet

	CLAIM	FACT
#1	*The plan is to fully integrate Grade 8 students with THS students, and mixing Grade 8 students with high school students is developmentally inappropriate.*	Fact: We are exploring all options from full integration to isolating Grade 8 students from the rest of the population. A Community Input Team will develop a comprehensive plan to be considered and approved by the District Transition Team. Community members will have an opportunity to weigh in on the options.
#2	*No one has looked at finances to see how much could be saved with school closures.*	Fact: Completing a cost-analysis was one of the first tasks undertaken, which was how we arrived at the $1.6 million projected savings. The cost-analysis was conservative and includes savings from positions such as administrators, guidance counselors, nurses, custodians, etc.
#3	*The school closure and consolidation plan is all about money.*	Fact: Finances are only part of the equation. The current school closure and consolidation plan is about two things: (1) finances; and (2) educational equity. Students in some of our schools do not have access to the same programs and facilities that other students do. Safety issues and handicapped accessibility are also major concerns. The school closure and consolidation plan currently under consideration provides a cost-savings and a comprehensive PK–12 solution that is fair and equitable, improvingthe educational experiences of the students of Walker, Maxham, and Mulcahey.
#4	*There will be a significant increase in transportation expenses and significant overcrowding on high school buses.*	Fact: Our current busing contract is not based on mileage, it is based on the number of students riding the bus. Busing routes are being reconfigured, tiers are being examined, and plans are in the works to keep transportation costs at a minimum and to address issues of overcrowding.
#5	*We are going to lose the middle school teaming concept if we send Grade 8 to THS.*	Fact: No changes have been made to the Grade 8 teaming concept. A Curriculum and Professional Development Community Input Team will be assembled to examine the curriculum and explore the most effective and developmentally appropriate instructional strategies for students in Grade 8.
#6	*We were told there was overcrowding at THS, which is why we voted for the Parker/THS project. Now we're being told that there's too much space. What happened?*	Fact: The enrollment projections from an earlier study in 2003 did not materialize. That study indicated a projected increase of 1,400 students. It was further anticipated that THS would be well over 2,300 students by 2010. These projections have not come to fruition, and 1,810 students are currently enrolled at THS. The NESDEC study found that we lost approximately 150 students during the past decade, and we are expected to lose 150 more in the next decade. The capacity of THS is 2,600 students, which means that there is room for approximately 800 more students.
#7	*Consideration should be given to closing a facility other than Walker School, since it is the only school in that part of the City.*	Fact: Consideration has been given to closing other schools, and detailed data are included in the Capacity and Utilization Study. The reason that Walker School is being considered for closure is because it is no longer eligible for school construction and renovation funds, and necessary upgrades include a $1 million roof, $50,000 in immediate temporary roof repairs, and extensive work to resolve issues of moisture, ventilation, windows, insulation, heating, cooling, electrical service, and sewer. In addition, there are safety and handicapped accessibility issues that are of concern. The needs of the other schools considered for closure were not as extensive and costly as those at Walker School.
#8	*There is enough room at Elizabeth Pole School to accommodate all of the students from one of the schools closing, thereby limiting the need to redistrict.*	Fact: There is not enough room to accommodate an entire school at Elizabeth Pole School. Space that used to exist is now being used for programs for students who were formerly placed out-of district, and for Title I students and those with special needs. Redistricting will need to occur to accommodate students and address issues of equity in the system.

community this upset, and the school closures and consolidations were the topic of conversation on every ball field, in every business, and in every hair salon. In the words of one administrator, the forum was going to be "a bloodbath."

I knew it would be a challenge, and against the better judgment of some members of my administrative team, I went ahead and organized the forum. Shortly after the school board voted to move ahead with our school reforms, I organized a community forum, a "Grade 8 to the High School Transition Night," and well over three hundred fifty upset parents and caregivers were in attendance. In preparation for this event, I had our media teacher work with his students to develop a video titled "A Day in the Life of an Eighth Grader," and I asked the teacher to interview students and fellow teachers, following eighth grade pilot students through a typical day. Prior to sending the eighth grade to the high school, we did a voluntary pilot, giving approximately one hundred and twenty eighth graders an opportunity to enroll in high school. These pioneers spent a semester at the high school prior to our "Grade 8" community forum, and the positive, upbeat aspects of having eighth graders in the high school was an important part of the story that we wanted to share. I also asked that the video production team home in on those honest challenges that might make the transition a struggle for students and teachers. I then invited ten panelists including students, teachers, parents, administrators, school board designees, and community members who were in favor of the transition, or once opposed to it, to talk about the reasons why it made sense. Next, I moderated a question-and-answer forum with the audience, enlisting the help of my panelists. This forum signaled to the community that the transition was going to happen, and it gave them the opportunity to ask tough questions and confront others and me on the issue. It also gave my administrators and school board a chance to hear the public concerns and a better understanding of what work needed to be done to demonstrate our responsiveness.

It is reasonable for a public interested in maintaining the status quo to develop a deep mistrust for any leader interested in school reform. A way to overcome those feelings is to talk candidly about what you hope to accomplish and why.

People may still be skeptical, but if you are sincere and have good reasons behind your decisions, your students and school community will feel it. If you are playing tricks and trying to execute school reforms, such as school closures, to try to get rid of teachers who are underperforming, stay home. The public will quickly see through your scheme, and a bloodbath in that case is the likely outcome. In our case, the public was very passionate but appreciative of the way we handled the situation. Fortunately, the plain-clothes officer that my school board insisted on hiring for the evening was not needed to keep the peace, but he did provide us with lots of positive feedback about our handling of such a controversial community issue.

Step 7: Develop a Communication Plan

The last step in the community input team process is developing a communication plan. In school reform, it is essential to share what is working and what is not, and to hold yourself accountable by telling the public what it is that you intend to do about the situation. As shown in appendix 6.1, we developed a monthly District Transition Team Newsletter to keep the community abreast of the changes that were being made as a result of the DTT/CIT efforts. Among other things, the newsletter, disseminated both electronically and in hard copy, specifically addressed an issue that was problematic for many parents and caregivers of rising eighth graders: what would happen to their child's middle school graduation? We intended to do away with middle school graduation for a host of reasons, so parents did not necessarily get the answer they wanted to hear in this case; however, those who were involved in the CITs and DTT could attest that we had given the issue serious consideration, the DTT came to consensus on the issue, and we were able to communicate this decision to others.

Following the seven-step community input team process as a model for ushering in school reform helped me implement effective changes and lead my school community through some of the most significant challenges in our history, fortifying my relationships with my school board and school community in the process. They were proud of the way we had worked together to solve some serious challenges, and they were invested in the success of our reforms. It is not every day that a superintendent and school board members hear members of the public say, "I was wrong about that consolidation you put in place a few years ago, and moving the eighth grade to the high school was one of the best things that ever happened to my child." If this had been a comment we heard only once, we would be grateful, but my school board members and I hear this all the time. There is nothing that strengthens a superintendent–school board relationship more than enduring those formidable and challenging times and making a positive and lasting difference for the children in your schools.

APPENDIX 6.1 TPS Transitions Newsletter Excerpt

FREQUENTLY ASKED QUESTIONS BY STUDENTS AND PARENTS

1. I am a new parent. How and why was the decision to send Gr. 8 students to THS made, and was it due to the economic situation?

Financial challenges had a lot to do with the decision, and issues of equity also played a major role. We spent over a year discussing school consolidations and closures, and there are many benefits (see "CLASS" article on pg. 1). For more information about the decision-making process, please visit www.tauntonschools.org and click "Transitions."

2. Last year several students participated in the Gr. 8 Pilot Program. What worked, what didn't, and is participation next year voluntary?

Please see "The Gr. 8 Pilot: What Worked and What We Learned" (pg. 2) for some highlights of successes and challenges. We will also hear a first-person account from a student, a parent, and a teacher in a feature story in the April edition of the newsletter. The Gr. 8 Pilot Program ends this year, and participation is no longer voluntary. All Gr. 8 students will attend THS next year.

3. Middle school students currently fit in the middle schools. Do we need to send Gr. 8 to THS?

Yes. The decision to move Gr. 8 to THS was based upon a careful analysis of demographics and capacity utilization studies. There are currently an estimated 800—1,000 empty seats at THS. It is our goal to get each of the schools in our system at Planned Operating Capacity, (POC) so our students can achieve at their highest levels in a setting that is educationally appropriate and conducive to learning. We have more work to do in this area, but we are well on our way.

4. There is a developmental gap between a 13 year old and a senior in high school. Is there any research about the academic, psychological and social effects on students who have made similar transitions?

We know that change is hard, and developmental gaps exist among students no matter the grade configuration or setting. To combat these challenges, THS established a successful Senior Student Mentor Program to encourage positive interactions between Gr. 8 students and upperclassmen, which will continue. Gr. 8 Pilot students indicate that this support was invaluable. Upperclassmen developed a sense of responsibility and ownership for making the Gr. 8 students' experience a positive one. In addition, administrators and THS guidance counselors have personally visited six (6) high schools that recently consolidated with their middle schools to find out more about the developmental needs of the students. There is no evidence to suggest that placing students in a building with upper classmen will have a harmful effect on students. In fact, what we have learned is quite the opposite; schools have reported that students tend to be positively influenced by the presence of older peers.

5. What will my child's schedule look like next year, and when will s/he sign up for classes?

THS has a 4 x 4 Block Schedule, which means that students have four 84 minute periods per day, per semester. Gr. 8 Pilot students and teachers say that having fewer courses to manage at once has eased the transition. Students will sign up for courses in March.

END OF YEAR ACTIVITIES FOR GRADES 7 & 8

One of the most frequently asked questions concerns the participation of Gr. 7 students in the Gr. 8 graduation ceremonies. This decision has been carefully weighed by the District Transition Team and middle school leaders, and we will hold separate events to honor students.

Gr. 8 students will participate in traditional graduation ceremonies. Gr. 7 students will take part in a special culminating event to celebrate their accomplishments and transition to THS. These ceremonies will be based at the respective middle schools and designed to fit the unique culture of each middle school. Gr. 7 students will have an opportunity to celebrate their academic, athletic, and social achievements together, and this special recognition will be accompanied by a dance and other fun activities. More information coming soon from your building principal.

SAVE THE DATES!

Grade 7 Recognition/Dance
June 16, 2011 (Tentative Date)

Grade 8 Graduation Ceremonies
June 21, 2011 (Tentative Date)

CHAPTER SEVEN

If Not Home, Then Make It the Place You Long to Be

Cultural patterns are highly enduring, have a powerful impact on performance, and shape the ways people think, act and feel.

—DEAL & PATTERSON, 1999

IN THIS BUSINESS, it matters where you live and where you leave your heart. In many cases today, superintendents reside outside the school communities they lead, which can put them at a relational disadvantage from the start. The role of residency in establishing a strong school culture should not be underestimated. School cultures are "complex webs of traditions and rituals" that are shaped when all members of a school community work through crises and accomplishments together. According to Deal and Peterson, these cultural patterns "are highly enduring, have a powerful impact on performance, and shape the ways people think, act and feel."[1]

If you are a superintendent whose personal life and experiences exist outside that complex cultural web, and you are unaccustomed to the traditions and rituals of the school community you lead, your school board and others may see you in a different light. You can pretend that the school culture is not influenced

EIGHT WAYS TO CREATE CONNECTIONS EVEN AT A DISTANCE

1. Embrace the culture and heritage.
2. Partner with area businesses.
3. Hire locals and let them advance.
4. Connect with clergy.
5. Make friends with the mayor.
6. Unite with your unions.
7. Identify your community's unique attributes.
8. Show up when they least expect you.

by where you lay your head at night, but the truth is, in most cases, it matters a great deal to school board members and your constituents. Accepting this way of thinking can help you countermand the negative impacts that arise when you encounter the "you're not one of us" mentality, and it can help you think strategically about the steps you will take to endear yourself to your school community.

If given a choice, many school board members will tell you that they prefer to hire a superintendent who lives or wants to live in their community. Most will probably tell you that it makes perfect sense for the top wage earner in their school system to live in the city or town that issues his paycheck. If you are an aspiring superintendent, you should recognize the advantage to be gained by letting prospective school boards know that your are willing to live where you lead, and you may be able to use residency as a bargaining chip to demonstrate a high level of commitment to your potential employer. After all, what better way for you to convince a school board that you are fully committed to the job than to promise to live, work, and play in the same city or town?

Currently, only five school systems in the Commonwealth of Massachusetts have such residency requirements for superintendents,[2] and the Maine legislature recently voted down a proposal to require residency.[3] While the trend appears to be moving away from residency requirements, the reality is that it still matters. School board members are elected public servants who run for office because they want to make a difference for the children in their own community. Time is precious, and school board members give theirs away freely and often with little reward. They want to make their schools better for their children and the sons and daughters and relatives of their neighbors—and they have every right to expect this same level of commitment from their superintendent of schools. While legitimate realities like the current housing market and the superintendent shortage call into question the need for a residency requirement, many school boards have not lost their desire for the superintendent to be an integral part of their rituals, traditions, and culture.

When a superintendent knows a city or town and appreciates and values its unique qualities, it matters to everyone, but proving loyalty to a school community takes hard work and commitment. For example, in my school system, I know that school retirees—people who also happen to be very important to me—are an active and connected group in the city, and I make it a point to reach out and include them in our school functions. They have been my guests at important events, including the grand opening of our new student-run café. More recently, on my teachers' opening day, I surprised educators during my opening remarks by having our former employees run out on the stage to help us celebrate, and the retirees, representing more than five hundred years of service to the school system, nearly brought down the house! A school community thrives when its members know and feel a connection to their superintendent or school leader; if you are someone who is interested in them and appreciates their history, your school community will feel connected to you. When you take the time to get to know all people in the community better, you will convince others that you respect and value their culture.

Students benefit from a superintendent who invests in their community's values and beliefs, and with over eight thousand two hundred students in my school system, I do my best to make sure they know me well. Young people are comfortable and know they can drop by my office, send me tweets and e-mails, and approach me with all sorts of interesting questions, such as "Can I be your intern?" or "Do you think I'll get a job as a special education teacher if I get a tattoo?" I have had students stop and say "hello" to me in restaurants in neighboring states, they recognize me at community celebrations like the annual lighting of the green, and they reach out to me for hugs at funerals. The reason is that my students see me interacting with their families and attending their local parades, sports and performing arts events, and community celebrations, and it matters to them. I may not live in the city, but my students know I believe in them, and they know I care. Through my decades in education, I have learned that when the adults in children's lives believe in them unconditionally, they always achieve far more than they would have without such support.

DOES A SUPERINTENDENT'S ZIP CODE REALLY MATTER?

I'm not going to lie. If relationship building is a priority for you (and by now I hope I have convinced you it should be if you want your reforms to last), the best arrangement for you is to live in the same community you lead. The proper zip code puts you at a definite advantage because it gives you a high level of credibility and instantaneous decision-making clout. How do I know this? I know this because I have *never* lived in the community that I lead, and I have had to work twice as hard to counteract the effect of this decision. I have closely observed the benefits of such an arrangement by watching my husband (who is also a superintendent) lead where he lives. These observations give me cause to believe that there is a positive advantage associated with residing in the same community in which you work, an observation my husband does not dispute. However, he is the first to remind me that while I enjoy a quiet commute home unwinding and listening to the sounds of deliriously soothing classical music, he is the one who gets stuck feeding and walking the dog, running to the grocery store, bumping into the occasional angry parent or two, making dinner, and shuttling the kids around to all their wrestling and soccer practices, sleepovers, and music lessons. On second thought, maybe living away from the community you lead does have its advantages!

Throughout the course of my career as a school leader, I have not lived where I led, but plenty of times I have longed to be a resident. One such time was during a recent city council meeting when I made a pitch for a new high school stadium. My school board commended me for putting forward a logical and convincing argument to fund a state-of-the-art stadium, one that is well built, durable, and designed to be a source of pride for the community. But in this business, compelling arguments are not always enough. We debated the extent to which the city can afford particular options for construction, and the council rightfully expressed concern about the impact of the new construction on taxpayers who had recently voted for a $112 million school renovation/construction project.

Although I had important information that helped influence the discussion (did you know a $500,000 project increase to get all the "bells and whistles" translates to just a little over $30,000 per year in the city's bond schedule, and with such a slight increase annually, doesn't it make more sense to do this right the first time?), it is in times like this that I long to live where I lead. It would have significantly bolstered my argument to be able to speak as both superintendent *and* resident. When you live where you work, you speak with greater authority on the issues and make more compelling arguments, such as "I can tell you both as a superintendent and a taxpayer who supported the new school project that this is without a doubt the best option for the city, and here's why."

As it turns out, the city council voted to approve our request for a new stadium, and I believe it is fair to say that this result can be attributed in part to the strategies recommended in chapter 8 and elsewhere in this book, which have helped me forge strong connections with local officials and members of the community. You can overcome distance using some of the strategies in this chapter, but there is no denying that the countless leadership challenges like this would be far easier to manage if you were a resident in the same city or town in which you work. Some challenges that threaten to hit the taxpayers' pocket books are quickly met with a "Sure, it's easy for her to say we need a new stadium because she doesn't have to pay for it—we do!" And then there are those that involve significant cultural reforms like closing and consolidating schools when I have heard, "What does she care? She's going to make all these changes that we don't even want and then go somewhere else!" Living in the community you lead has its share of advantages, and it creates a "we're all in this together" mindset that can make the work a little less daunting, but living where you lead is not the only way to build strong connections and get things done.

CONNECTIONS AT A DISTANCE

Sometimes living in the same community you lead just is not possible, and you need practical strategies to overcome this disadvantage. Perhaps your partner has a job in another community, maybe you are caring for an ailing or aging family member and must remain close by, or a transition to another school would be highly disruptive for your child who is only a year or so from graduation. Whatever the circumstances, if you live away, you must find ways to counteract the community skepticism that is borne by distance, and establish a symbiotic relationship with your school board and your constituents if you want to make changes that last.

Regardless of the miles between your house and your office, you need to create similar connections that can withstand the miles and have a lasting impact on the community. If you are not resting your head on a comfy pillow in their city or town, you will need to do some work to show the school board that you are fully committed to their community and what matters most to them. Throughout my career, I have worked with school board members who are extremely easygoing and some who can be rather challenging. When I take the time to show them how much I care about them, their people, and the community they love—and not just their schools—it makes all the difference.

There are triumphs and tragedies in every city and town, and a sense of togetherness is developed as people share experiences in common. Community-building events can be both positive and negative, and in the city in which my school system resides, there have been many unifying experiences for me to connect with the people, such as the opening day of little league baseball, the fire that destroyed city hall, the 100th lighting of the green, and the death of a beloved local pastor. If you are a superintendent who lives away, you can easily miss (and allow yourself to miss) these important milestones, but your school board and school community need to know that you feel about them the same way that you would if they were your next-door neighbor. Now let's explore some specific strategies that you can use to create your own "connections at a distance" to communicate your commitment and show your school board you care.

IF YOU DON'T LIVE THERE, GIVE TWICE THE CARE

Make no mistake: in my view, the best arrangement for you is to live where you lead. A community is defined as a "unified body of individuals," who share common interests, characteristics, and histories. If you are a superintendent who wants to create your own "connections at a distance" to influence your school board and shape school culture, you can take a series of actions. If you live outside the community and relationship building matters to you, schools are not your only job; your job also is to learn all that you can about the community and at least act like a resident. There are eight reliable methods you can use to build stronger relationships with your school board and help shape the climate: (1) embrace the culture and heritage; (2) partner with area businesses; (3) hire locals and let them advance; (4) connect with clergy; (5) make friends with the mayor; (6) unite with your unions; (7) identify your community's unique attributes; and (8) show up when they least expect you. These strategies are applicable to those of you who reside in the municipality or live outside the city or town in which you work.

Step 1: Embrace the Culture and Heritage

Every school community has a unique culture and heritage that you must know. My school system happens to be in a city with a large Cape Verdean population, and many of my employees and some school board members are of Portuguese descent. Their culture and heritage are important to them, as they should be, and I have spent time learning all that I can by reading, researching, and experiencing their values and beliefs. I have read books and attended lectures to learn more about the history and immigration of the Portuguese population to the city. I have eaten chorizo and linguica, and I have attended more than one "meat on a stick," a term the locals use to describe a Portuguese event where families get together to visit and cook large chunks of meat on skewers over hot coals. The Consul of Portugal visits our schools regularly and knows who I am. I have spent time talking to my custodians, teachers, and staff about what it was like to flee Faial Island in the 1960s with their families when the earthquake struck, and I have attended the funerals of my employees and their loved ones spoken entirely in Portuguese. Some share stories with me about recent trips back home to the Azores, and from time to time I even get mementos like a beautiful picture book about the homeland of an employee, who wanted to share with me his journey back to his native country. While I may not have the same set of experiences as those in the community in which I lead, I have embraced their culture and heritage in ways that matter to them, and this matters to my school community.

Step 2: Partner with Area Businesses

Students win when school leaders collaborate with business partners. Business owners often look for ways to give back to the community, and the better you know them, the more support they will give your students and your schools. Joining civic organizations such as the Rotary Club and Kiwanis are good ways to make connections and meet potential partners. It is also useful for you to dream up unique school projects that will give area businesses an opportunity to connect with you in special ways. I recently partnered with two local banks to improve our schools; one business partner generously restored the seats in our high school auditorium at a cost of $75,000, and the other agreed to fund a $90,000 creative project that our students designed. Our advanced high school students in Drafting and Computer-Aided Design (CAD) courses developed their ideal set of graphic design plans for a new and improved Tiger Tent Café (our current café is quite literally a tent behind the high school). The teacher instructed them to create their ideal restaurant, one that would be economical and functional for their peers in the Culinary Arts program and in keeping with our vision to do more outreach to the senior citizens in our community.

When the designs were complete, the teacher invited the headmaster and me to see the student presentations. The student work was more impressive than I would have imagined, and I promised to include a new restaurant in our district goals and find the funding to make their dreams a reality. We selected the top three designs, and I asked the students to present to the school board at a televised meeting. They explained their designs and discussed sophisticated concepts such as the need to comply with the Americans with Disabilities Act (ADA), and how they were able to creatively meet these specifications and stay on budget by coming up with innovative ideas like tying into the existing plumbing.

Next, I pitched their idea to local businesses, and I then asked the mayor if he wanted to work with me to convince businesses to allocate the resources to make the student designs a reality. We were fortunate to get the backing of a local bank, which presented an oversized check for $30,000, the first of three we will receive over the next three years. This was one of the most rewarding school–business partnerships yet in my career because students were central to the initiative. The project helped forge strong connections between the schools and the community, and it is hard to say who was more excited—the students, the business partners, or the school board and me.

Step 3: Hire Locals and Let Them Advance

One of the worst mistakes I have seen superintendents make, especially those who consider themselves school reformers, is to resist hiring locals. They hire exclusively from the outside and make the case that locals are too entrenched to do what is right, all they want is the status quo, and they are incapable of change. One reason school boards like to hire locals as superintendents is that doing so generally guarantees some longevity and at least some knowledge of what matters to a community; plus they can reasonably anticipate that the superintendent, also a local, may be willing to give jobs to residents in their community.

To suggest that there is not one single resident capable of helping you achieve your vision for the school system is short-sighted and narrow-minded. As the superintendent of schools, you are typically the largest employer in the city or town. If you hire only from outside the system, you are denying opportunity to the community and the taxpayers who pay your salary. During these times of educational reform, a wonderful way to build the confidence and trust of your school board and community is to hire the talented locals (and you can always find some out there) who attended your schools and live in the community. Later, when they have proven themselves in the position, tap them for job promotions and let them advance. Locals care deeply about their community, and unlike some employees eager to advance outside the system, any investment you make in a resident is money well spent. They will stay loyal to the schools and their city or town, and when you need to make significant changes, there is no one better to have at your side than the people who have the history, relationships, and influence in the community and can help sell your ideas, making your schools better for the students you serve.

Step 4: Connect with Clergy

When they are not with family or at work, where do your students, parents, and employees spend the majority of their time, and in whom do they trust and confide? Connecting with clergy is an often-overlooked relationship-building strategy that enables you to make connections with your school community. They can not only help you build relationships but also offer an important source of support when you encounter the inevitable struggles that come with the job. Those in your school community who encounter life's challenges are likely to turn to a deacon, minister, pastor, priest, rabbi, or another member of the clergy for support. If this person to whom they are turning has already developed a relationship with you in your community and knows and believes in you, this relationship will make a difference to those who know and trust him.

A word of advice: reach out to your clergy before you encounter a struggle. I reached out to mine during a challenging time shortly after I took my first superintendency, which was the way that we first came to know one another. Forging these connections early, before there are challenges, helps so that the clergy will have a chance to know you for who you are and what you are trying to accomplish. I had a friendship with a bishop in our community who, prior to his passing, sent me a tweet acknowledging that I was the first female to lead my school system. He was a great person, and I believe that his support of me may have positively influenced some of the relationships I have been able to form, especially with the young women of color from his church who attend my schools.

Step 5: Make Friends with the Mayor

In many urban school systems, mayors lead school boards, and it is their job to look out for the interests of both the city and the schools. In these cases, superintendents have a narrower scope of responsibility that is, in many ways, higher stakes, and natural tensions can arise when they focus solely on the schools and do not take into consideration the needs of the city. Flexibility is the key to making this relationship work, and my role as a school leader is to advocate for ways to make education better for our students. This sometimes translates to requests in the form of additional funding that not every mayor can support. My job as superintendent is to acquire the necessary resources to adequately meet the needs of the students I serve, a role that is sometimes at odds with a mayor's point of view or his financial situation.

Being superintendent requires a delicate balance between advocacy and understanding, and you would not be doing your job if you did not look out for the interests of the school system and the students. By the same token, when I make a financial request to the mayor or I advocate publicly for more school funding, I make every effort to recognize the city's hardships and financial challenges and the mayor's many positive contributions, as well as his desire to do more to support education. I also find ways to generate creative revenue streams, so I am not always asking for resources, but I also am giving back to the city. For example, a few years ago in my school community, the city hall burned to the ground, and while I never shirk my obligation to advocate for funding to improve education for the children in my school community, I am ever mindful of the challenges our city officials face, with dwindling resources, as they work to restore a building that was once the heart of the downtown. After the tragedies in Newtown, Connecticut, school and municipal leaders throughout the nation were reeling. There was a public outcry to improve safety and security in schools, and city officials went on record stating that this issued needed to be addressed right away in our schools, but there was a problem—the city had no money to cover the costs of the needed technology, infrastructure, and upgrades. Instead of pointing the finger and blaming the city for not producing the funding, we wrote grants and the school board authorized the use of other revenue streams to secure additional safety equipment. These collaborative efforts can go a long way in building a solid relationship.

Natural tensions arise when superintendents do their job and advocate for the schools and students, and mayors and municipal leaders must do their job to look out for the interests of the entire city. As a school leader, you should find ways to partner with the mayor on important issues that matter to you and the community. In the past, mayors and town managers have asked me to serve on town/school efficiency committees and building committees, organize special events including hosting President Clinton at one of our schools, participate in historical celebrations that matter to the community like Liberty and Union Day, and help organize antidrug campaigns. Good superintendents know that for a school system to be strong, it needs to be situated in a healthy, thriving community. Strong relationships between the mayor or municipal leader and the superintendent increase the likelihood that education will be taken seriously and students will get what they need.

Step 6: Unite with Your Unions

Absolute authority and autocratic rule given to any one individual is a dangerous thing, yet certain school reformers seem perturbed by the slightest bit of interference from employees or school community members who are the recipients of these reforms. While the antilabor sentiment was recently at a fever pitch in some parts of the nation, making it fashionable for school reformers to discount and disrespect unions, taking this stance is a mistake if you are trying to make connections in your community. Labor unions have been around a long time, and they were created for good reason—to protect workers against the exploitation of an unscrupulous leader. Even if members of your school board or community are not not thrilled with their local labor unions, if you are a superintendent—especially one "from away"—who cannot get along with employees and your union, whose side do you think your school board will take?

Beyond that, establishing a close and trusting relationship with union leaders is essential if you are hoping to make significant changes as superintendent. In all the school systems in which I have worked, I have established strong ties with union leadership by respecting their knowledge and taking a genuine interest in my employees' well-being. While we do not always agree, there is always an open dialogue, and I try to listen and learn from their points of view. Any change is far less effective without the buy-in from the individuals who are expected to implement the change, so you need unions to help make your reforms last. Our relationship is a healthy one because the union leadership is not afraid to speak up, and I am not afraid to share my views. School systems advance when superintendents and unions work together, and our strong partnership has led to productive labor-management collaborations resulting in innovations, such as one of the first district models of inclusion in our state. These outcomes would not have been possible without a close relationship with the union president and leadership.

Step 7: Identify Your Community's Unique Attributes

Every city or town has a unique identity that reflects shared values, and if you live away, you need to be especially attuned to knowing what matters most to the community that you lead. In my school community, mentoring and adult literacy are very much a part of the city's identity. Each year, I show my support for the efforts that are valued by the community leaders; for example, I participate in annual walkathons to show my support for helping adults develop the literacy skills they need to achieve more, and I volunteer each year to mentor a student, helping him graduate and go on to college. I do this because it is personally rewarding for me, and the community takes great pride in these events.

Step 8: Show Up When They Least Expect You

I look for opportunities to be part of the fabric of the community, and I make it a point to show up where and when people least expect me. People expect me to be at school events, but they do not expect me to show up in the community, so I do just that—a community garden event that is important to a school board member, a local celebration, a parade, a funeral. I am the superintendent of schools in a municipality that calls itself "The Christmas City." Last year was the 100th lighting of the Taunton Green, and residents showed up in droves to celebrate this festive occasion, so I made sure I was there to celebrate with them. I have been involved in many community events, but one of my favorite times was when I joined other residents in the community to create the "largest human Christmas tree." I dragged my family out in the cold, and we stood huddled together in red and green plastic ponchos with other residents to break a record celebrated in the *Guinness Book of World Records*. I may not live in the city, but after braving negative thirty degrees, not many could say I don't care.

As you think about the best ways to create connections at a distance, keep in mind that these strategies can also be useful if you live in the same community you lead. The important point to all of this is that you need to find ways to let people know that you respect them, and you care about their future and their past. Theodore Roosevelt said, "Nobody cares how much you know until they know how much you care," and that is one of my favorite quotes of all times because it has so many implications for teaching and learning. Your content knowledge may be off the charts, but if are unable to connect with a community and its people, you will not get far when it comes to transforming your schools.

CHAPTER EIGHT

Communication That Counts

A superintendent is much more likely to have expertise in finance than in communications, yet lack of communications sophistication is the one thing most likely to shorten his or her tenure.

—National School Public Relations Association, 2007

STRONG COMMUNICATION SKILLS are a must for any chief executive officer, and these skills are particularly vital when you are a superintendent of schools. The way in which you interact with your school board often determines your success or failure in the job; however, few if any resources are available to teach you the skills you need to communicate on a meaningful level when you are trying to build relationships with your school board. The communication skills that you need today are increasingly more sophisticated, yet you are hard-pressed to develop expertise in these skills when you have no exposure to the advanced communication techniques that will help you forge stronger bonds with your school board. To that end, I will describe several communication strategies that I use regularly, which may be of use to you. They have helped me be a more effective leader and strengthen my relationships with my school board.

> THE RULE OF ALL
>
> **SIX COMMUNICATION STRATEGIES TO BUILD LONG-LASTING SCHOOL BOARD RELATIONSHIPS**
>
> 1. Differentiate school board communication.
> 2. Frame the problem and give them cover.
> 3. Share the good, the bad, the ugly.
> 4. Develop a role for the board in times of crisis.
> 5. Be their voice.
> 6. Use "mid-course correction" to keep relationships intact.

Before we delve into these strategies, let's explore the *types* of communication strategies I am recommending in this chapter. Communication is defined as "the act of transmitting information from one source to another."[1] It can be verbal or nonverbal, formal or informal, and conveyed in a variety of ways (by telephone, text, post, e-mail, fax, or in person). Body language also plays a role in communication in that how you deliver a message can be just as important as the content itself. These are all foundational skills that you may have acquired in your undergraduate classes or through your life experiences, but the types of communication I am recommending in this chapter go beyond this level. As superintendent, you need a sophisticated yet practical set of communication strategies you can rely on to include others, manage crises, build trust, and strengthen your superintendent–school board relationships.

THE RULE OF ALL (ROA)

Communication strategies that build relationships begin with an inclusive mindset that attends to the needs of all school board members. Some superintendents (and board members alike) have been known to "count the votes," a practice that a former superintendent I know calls the "Rule of Five." While some school leaders consider this approach effective, I can think of few approaches that are more antithetical to building lasting relationships with your school board. Relationships quickly devolve into transactions when superintendents "take the pulse" of the school board to determine how each member will vote and whether a motion will pass. My advice to you is to try your hand instead at what I call the "Rule of All."

The "Rule of All" means you do your best to set aside your concern with the outcome of a vote, instead focusing on the concerns of your school board members. What I have observed when my colleagues use the "Rule of Five" is that the person counting the votes typically begins by making an assessment of each school board member's position to gauge the amount of work that will be required to make a decision go her way. If the school leader wants to adopt a new curriculum, implement a new initiative, or build a new school, and a majority vote of the eight-member school board is necessary, all she needs is a total of five votes to succeed. It might be obvious that the superintendent has four school board members solidly in her corner, which means she can focus her efforts on just one of the outliers (preferably a fence-sitter who may be more easily swayed than one who is in strong opposition). This approach might get her the majority vote and what she wants for now, but the "Rule of Five" victory is short-lived. Eventually, this strategy creates tension, breeds mistrust, and sends the wrong message to school board members who do not necessarily feel the same way that the superintendent does about a given issue.

When you practice the "Rule of Five," you effectively write off school board members, which has obvious implications when you are attempting to build solid superintendent–school board relationships. Some school leaders I know say, "Oh well, that's politics," and they use the strategy as an easy and effective way to win. It feels a bit like dirty pool to me, an underhanded approach that erodes relationships in the long run. My advice to you is to stop worrying about the final vote and instead invest your effort and energy into helping people understand what is riding on the outcome of a vote and why a particular decision is good for the school system and your students. The work is harder, but it will make you a better leader, and it will make your school board respect you more.

When you practice the "Rule of All," investing in every school board member, you are more likely to get what you want in the end. Developing a shared understanding between you and your school board takes more effort, but in the process you will learn more about what matters most to members of your team. School board members will feel included and not alienated, you will gain their confidence and respect, and in so doing you will see your relationships with the school board and their relationships with one another develop and grow.

COMMUNICATION STRATEGIES THAT BUILD BETTER BOARD RELATIONS

As you carry the "Rule of All" philosophy into your work with the school board, you can use certain communication strategies to advance your relationship-building efforts. School board members want a superintendent who is a skilled communicator at the helm of their schools; they want a leader who is articulate, writes well, and possesses strong interpersonal skills. These themes are prevalent in the literature on desirable leadership qualities,[2] yet little has been written on how you can develop the sophisticated communication skills needed to improve your relationships with school board members. I have used a number of advanced communication skills to build superintendent–school board relationships that others may employ as well, including (1) differentiate school board communication; (2) frame the problem and give them cover; (3) share the good, the bad, the ugly; (4) develop a role for the board in times of crisis; (5) be their voice; and (6) use "mid-course correction" to keep relationships intact.

Step 1: Differentiate School Board Communication

Communication with your school board can be problematic because each board member has his own preference and style for how information should be transmitted and received. Some school board members appreciate e-mails, some prefer daily phone calls, others prefer text, some want face-to-face discussions, and still others settle for any and all modes of communication you wish to use. School board members have their own work schedules and obligations to manage, limiting the time in which they can communicate with you. Natural tensions around superintendent–school board communication are not uncommon, but these conflicts tend to dissipate when you take the time to learn your school board's communication preferences.

EXHIBIT 8.1 Differentiating communication with your school board

DIFFERENTIATE COMMUNICATION WITH YOUR SCHOOL BOARD					
NAME	PREFERRED MODE OF COMMUNICATION				PREFERRED TIME OF DAY
	E-mail	Face-to-Face	Phone	Text	
Fred Jones	X	X			any
Doreen Cormier	X	X	X	X	9–5 p.m.
Allison James		X	X		after 6 p.m.
Steve Davidson	X	X	X	X	5–7 a.m.; 2–5 p.m.
Mark Jones	X	X	X	X	any
Fiona Caron	X	X	X		7–9 a.m.
Pat Peterson	X	X	X		7–10 a.m.
Owen Cross	X		X		9–5 p.m.
Harrison Taylor		X		X	any

If you are a superintendent or school leader who is using one primary form of communication with your board, you may want to rethink your practices. Tailoring the communication to the needs of your school board is important to the work you will do together. As you can see in exhibit 8.1, I map out the communication preferences of all school board members, including their preferred modes of communication and the times of day that work best for each member. While you should do your best to honor these preferences, sometimes only a personal touch will do. If I anticipate that a certain issue will generate a lot of questions, I place a call to each board member explaining all the details of the situation as I know them, within reason, extending an offer to meet individually with any school board member who wishes to further discuss.

Superintendents and school boards often encounter challenges when it comes to communication, and finding ways to avoid surprises is an area of concern that is often addressed in superintendent–school board norms and beliefs protocols. Certain types of communication can be problematic for school boards; for instance, I have worked with more than one school board member who believes e-mails are a poor form of communication for anyone to use at any time. My view is that e-mails work well in certain situations and for certain individuals; however, I do agree that some issues should never be shared through e-mail, such as a serious allegation, a lawsuit, or a dangerous situation in your schools. When I do use e-mail, I frequently include reminders to school board members to avoid a "reply to all" or any type of deliberation in deference to our state's Open Meeting Law derived from the Sunshine Act, a federal law that demands transparency in government.

To help those school board members for whom e-mail seems to be problematic, I have shared communications from the attorney general, demonstrating that e-mail is permissible in certain circumstances, and I let board members know they can opt out of the e-mails that I send if receiving them makes them uncomfortable. Sharing the communication preferences of all board members with those who oppose one form of communication or another can also help; this way, they can see you care about their preferences, understanding that what works best for one does not necessarily work best for others. Concerns tend to diminish when school board members know they get to decide on their preferred modes of communication, and they know you want to converse with them in the way that best meets their needs.

Step 2: Frame the Problem and Give Them Cover

Another effective communication strategy that you can use is to frame complex challenges for school board members and give them cover. School board members are vulnerable to a public that is quite unforgiving at times. When decisions are made, citizens often take their dissatisfaction out on the school board members because they do not have the authority to fire the superintendent. When you are engaged in school reform efforts, you run the risk of losing your job if a school board does not approve of the decisions you make or your leadership style, but a superintendent can take some comfort in knowing that it takes the agreement of a school board majority for this to happen. School board members, on the other hand, are elected officials, and each difficult decision that is made could cost them votes at election time. I have worked in several districts in which there are no term limits and school board members have served for decades. For many, the school board is their life's work, and when we are working on a school reform that is a hard sell and the public is discontented, it matters.

In chapter 6, you learned about the community input team process, a relationship-building strategy that I developed when we closed schools, repurposed a middle school, and put all eighth grade students in the high school. As you might imagine, this was a trying time for my school board members who had lived in the community all their lives. Their friends, family, and neighbors who had different hopes and dreams for their children were angry (a stage in the grieving process), and the school board members were inundated with complaints and concerns. I spent many hours talking through these issues and helping school board members anticipate what to expect and how we might deal with it, as we moved closer to enacting our plan. I also thought about the ways that I could deflect some of the anger being directed toward my school board. I wrote a letter in their defense and read it publicly at a meeting during our school closure and consolidation efforts. The public redirected its anger at me for a time, and the communication gave the school board some cover, helping us successfully transition our students to a new school configuration that was more equitable for all.

Step 3: Share the Good, the Bad, the Ugly

Sharing good news is easy, but when you do, be sure to give credit where credit is due. The school board almost always has a role in something positive that has happened in the school system, and you could not do your job without board members. When our dropout scores were cut in half, I publicly reminded the school community that this success was attributed to many who were invested in the work, including the school board members who were dissatisfied with our dropout data. This was an issue we addressed through our district goals because we knew our children deserved more. Every school board member wants to make a difference, and taking the time to share the good they do, acknowledging their contributions, is something every school leader should do.

Although sharing the good news can be easy, sharing the not-so-good news can be a challenge. In this day and age when distrust of anyone in a position of authority is at an all-time high, and support for public education is at an all-time low, it is understandable that most school leaders prefer to share the positive stories that reflect well on their leadership and the school system. Although doing so may feel counterintuitive, you also should share "the bad and the ugly" in your work. This is something that is not always pleasant to do, but I have tried to practice it regularly in my leadership through the years. If you are an urban superintendent, you will need to manage conflicts and crises. When my school system was under fire for accusations involving teacher misconduct, the mishandling of a particular situation, a serious incident involving dangerous weapons or drugs in school, or some other scandalous event that had happened (or was rumored to have happened), I considered it my responsibility to let my school board and school community know. Although it is tempting, I do not allow myself to get away with sharing only the good information that happens in this line of work, and I believe my school board members and school community appreciate my forthrightness. Sharing the good, the bad, and the ugly is an honest approach that builds trust and helps school board and school community members develop confidence in you.

Step 4: Develop a Role for the Board in Times of Crisis

An entire book could be written on how to communicate effectively with a school board during a crisis, but this book is focused on communication that helps superintendents build stronger relationships with their school boards. Therefore, the most important advice I can give you is in times of crisis, you need to include your school board. I know superintendents who withhold information from their school boards because they consider it their job to handle all administrative tasks (which it is), and they fear that if they share anything with the school board, the details will "leak out" in the public (which they sometimes do). When you do not give school board members a role during the school district's most challenging times, you unintentionally alienate them from your team. If you take a hard line on issues like this, you can lose more in the end, as school board members may translate this subtle form of rejection as a lack of trust in them, which in turn can negatively impact superintendent–school board relations. While these concerns are valid, your deliberate approach for enlisting school board members in crisis communications goes a long way in minimizing potential risk and maintaining a respectful and harmonious relationship with the school board.

Like it or not, school board members are out in the community every day fielding questions from a curious citizenry at soccer games, restaurants, and grocery stores. You can pretend you are the only one hearing the stories, but this could not be further from the truth. The public thinks that all school board members know what is happening in schools at all times, so board members may feel embarrassed when you cut them out of important communications. It is just as important for you to keep board members in the loop as it is for a school leader to address the media during a school emergency. Very often the details of a challenging situation or school crisis cannot be shared due to privacy laws related to personnel matters; however, school board members need to have at least a general sense of what is happening in the school system during these times.

Face-to-Face Communication in a Crisis

An effective way I involve my school board in crisis management is by following a multistep approach. First, I provide the school board with a general overview of the issue; for instance, I might explain that an educator has been accused of hitting a child. Next, I explain that I am working with law enforcement and legal counsel on the issue. It is important to keep in mind that your school board has financial oversight for all matters and lawyers cost money, so they need to be apprised. Then I let the school board know that I can answer questions generally, but I am not at liberty to disclose the name of a student, the school, or the accused because all employees, unless they are proven guilty, have a right to privacy on matters such as these. Finally, if the school board presses for more information,

I give a firm but gentle reminder that I have shared what I can tell them, and the less they know, the better off they are. This protocol gives the school board enough information to answer questions that may arise in the community, but it limits the amount of detail that could encroach upon an employee's rights, put the school board in the middle of the controversy, or get you in hot water for violating someone's privacy.

Written Communication in a Crisis

Most school leaders know how to handle a crisis, but they do not always consider the school board's role in crisis management. Your school board members are like a battalion of public servants who can be instrumental in helping you get your message out to the public, stabilizing the school community in trying times. Tragic and unfortunate situations can trigger emotional public reactions, and school board members may need your advice and guidance. As their superintendent, and the lead teacher in the system, you should not assume that all board members know how to react in a crisis. They may need you to coach them on how to respond to rumors, how to deal with upset neighbors, and how to handle other challenging situations. If time permits, you can brainstorm talking points with your school board, or you can offer suggestions for how the school board can respond to the public during an emergency. When rumors run rampant, school board members can be instrumental in allaying the fears and concerns of the public that can quickly spin out of control without effective communication strategies in place.

If you need to get a crisis communication out quickly about a serious incident that may spin out of control in the media, it may help to do the following: (1) have your administrative assistant place quick calls to all school board members to let them know an important message is on the way, explaining you will follow up with a phone call as soon as you can; (2) draft the communication and get right to the point; (3) keep the information as factual as possible; (4) anticipate the questions your school board members might be asked by the public; (5) outline possible responses the school board members can use when questioned by the public; (6) reread your message and imagine it is going to be printed in your local newspaper; (7) promise to call or discuss in person and answer any questions; and (8) make the calls to all school board members as soon as you can. Involving your school board in times of crisis is an important strategy that communicates trust and respect and builds superintendent–school board relationships.

Step 5: Be Their Voice

Relationships develop when individuals unite around a common enemy, and that is a truism that has stood the test of time. Friendships deepen when allies battle the bullies together, teammates become closer when they play their rivals, and politicians who once ran in opposition unite when the opposing political party threatens to take control. School board members may have difficulty coalescing around a common purpose, but a good battle in defense of your school system can do wonders for school board morale. You should seek out opportunities to be your school board's voice and help them unite around the issues that matter most to them.

To be a good superintendent, you need a strong sense of the collective values of your school board. You need to know where they stand on certain issues, such as high stakes testing or educator evaluation. You have an opportunity to play an advocacy role based on the school board's collective values, and believe it or not, you can build relationships when you pen letters for them to local and state officials, like the one shown in appendix 8.1. My school board was passionate about public education being overburdened with too many initiatives, so they took a vote to have me write a letter to the commissioner on this matter. They were proud to have their efforts recognized by the legislature and organizations such as the Massachusetts Association of School Superintendents, and this was a great superintendent–school board unifier. If you want to strengthen your relationships with the school board, you should make it a priority to be their voice.

Step 6: Use "Mid-Course Correction" to Keep Relationships Intact

It is never too late to begin again. This is a lesson I try to instill in my administrators, and it is something I keep in mind when times get tough. Eventually in your role as superintendent, you will experience conflict with a school board member, or there will come a time when you are asked to do something you just cannot do. For most school leaders, these challenges happen during the first days on the job. Saying yes to every idea or giving in to every demand is not leadership; it is acquiescence. Knowing how to communicate during these challenging times is important to your survival and your ability to build stronger relationships with your school board. It is helpful to keep in the back of your mind that people may enjoy working with someone who rolls over on every issue, but no one respects a person who gives in each time. As seen in chapter 2, when it appears that the relationship has been derailed, it is a good idea for you to use a "mid-course correction" to right the situation. By simply sharing concerns with the school board in an open and honest way, or perhaps raising the issue during a leadership retreat, you can acknowledge your feelings, take ownership of the issues that you own, and find out from your school board what you can do to get things back on track.

SELF-EVALUATE TO COMMUNICATE

Even when school board members are intimately involved in a school system, it can be difficult for them to know about your daily work, and a self-evaluation can offer the school board members important insights into the type and quality of the work being done. The self-evaluation can also be useful in identifying the collective achievements of your school system and addressing areas in need of improvement. If you focus exclusively on your own accomplishments in the self-evaluation process, you may miss an opportunity to strengthen your relationship with the school board, and you may unnecessarily open yourself up to criticism from members. The self-assessment is a powerful tool to clear the air of any persistent and vexing leadership issues that continue to resurface. It is also an effective way for you to demonstrate your sincere commitment to continuous improvement, and your responsiveness to school board members' concerns, letting them know that you are working on areas that matter most to them and their constituents.

While it is typically not a requirement for you to write or share your self-reflection or self-assessment with the school board, I find this relationship-building practice useful. When you engage in self-evaluation (often as part of the formal evaluation process), you might begin with a long list of the accomplishments that occur each year, but how often do you share what did not work? Elmore said that "privacy of practice produces isolation; isolation is the enemy of improvement."[3] Successful superintendents who ask questions and reflect openly and honestly about their strengths *and* failures position themselves and their school system well for future success, gaining the trust, respect, and confidence of their school board.

Superintendents who are under constant public scrutiny are reluctant to share their leadership failures and what does not work, but who can blame them? You are frequently subjected to the relentless and personal attacks of critics who leave nasty messages with school staff, send biting e-mails, or post vicious blogs that portend your imminent failure and doom, disheartening even the most stalwart leader. Some of my colleagues have faced scathing criticisms during school board meetings, held in open session and televised, often by elected officials under pressure to show they are listening to a particular grievance from constituents. Why then would you or any school leader want to contribute to the pessimism and negativity surrounding your leadership by pointing out your own flaws and weaknesses?

There is an easy answer for this: if you don't do it, someone else will. Telling the truth is freeing, and while it may be counterintuitive to divulge to your school board those leadership traits or aspects of the work that need improvement, ironically, you will benefit from publicly sharing your flaws. Even the most seasoned leader is bound to encounter difficulty, and the sooner you face your weaknesses and admit that there is room to grow, the better your relationship with school board members will be. Not even a professional quarterback like Tom Brady of the New England Patriots can throw for 500 yards with no interceptions, and even if he could, he certainly would not have the ability to sustain this effort for a season, so why would you imagine that your year could go off without a hitch?

Self-evaluations can be powerful tools for genuine improvement or merely devices used to mask unsuccessful performance. You may be tempted to use the self-evaluation process to, in effect, write your own evaluation and neutralize any criticisms or negative feedback by members of the school board, but I advise against this. I know of a superintendent who completed a self-evaluation, including a lengthy list of impressive accomplishments that he attributed to his leadership, which he shared in a public school board meeting. He hinted at one aspect of his work that might be in need of improvement, but he added an escape clause and quickly discounted that this could even be considered an issue because the designation of his lowest performing school was in dispute and under review by the state.

The superintendent's disclaimer suggested that the school's status was expected to improve in the near future, so there was really no cause for concern. It is unlikely that the promise of a potential change in the school's status did much to dispel the legitimate concerns of the school community, as most would consider it problematic for any school in their system to be designated as one of the lowest performing in the state. More may have been gained if the superintendent had used the self-evaluation process as a way to explore the data, along with any of his own disappointments, failed attempts, frustrations, new ideas, and renewed commitments to improving the performance of this particular school. Using such an approach establishes you as a lead learner who is reflective and capable of making changes to advance the system, which will earn you the respect and trust of your school community and school board.

In this case the superintendent washed his hands of any responsibility and did not identify any areas in need of improvement, so a school board member did his work for him in a very public way. The school board member took the superintendent's self-reflection, posted it on a social media site, and asked for public comment. The public was only too willing to assist with this effort, and when it came time for the superintendent's evaluation, the school board member had a long list of issues that the superintendent had failed to address. The circumstances may have been different if the superintendent had included some of those items in his self-evaluation in the first place, or at least an in-depth exploration of the issue. At the very least, the superintendent would have been the person to identify the persistent problems that are worrisome for the majority of school community members and exist in many other school communities. If the superintendent had stated in his self-assessment that the designation as a lowest performing school was unfair, but there are still ways the school can improve, the school board member may have been less interested in making this issue about him and publicly exposing his flaws.

A straightforward, no-excuses approach helps you build trust with constituents and advance the system. As a superintendent in an urban school system myself, I have used a self-evaluation approach to balance our school system's progress with legitimate issues that need to be addressed. I begin by highlighting the advancements we have made in our schools, and I emphasize that these successes belong to everyone, including the school board, which is always true. Effective superintendents recognize that shared leadership is important, and they understand that their work involves creating collaborative experiences that build a culture of openness and respect, enabling a team to commit to a common vision and make decisions that are in the best interests of students.[4]

The self-evaluation should also include any of your leadership traits that need improvement or anything that does not work in the school system. I make certain that I include my leadership shortcomings and disappointments (and, believe me, there are many) because honesty builds trust, and I know that it is important for me to model for my staff my commitment to continuous improvement. I also consider the perspectives of my school board members, and I think back to discussions throughout the year, imagining what each member would say about my performance. This self-reflection process has been effective for me, and the result is a more truthful and realistic assessment of the district's achievements, as well as the areas in which I hope to improve. As you can see in exhibit 8.2, I was able to identify in my self-evaluation the future efforts I hoped to undertake, and signal to the school board my thoughts on priorities that we should collectively establish in the district.

In this self-evaluation, I critiqued my instructional leadership, and I expressed disappointment that my efforts in the previous year produced only surface-level changes. However, pointing out my flaws did not negatively impact my relationship with the school board; in fact, my relationship with the school board improved as a result. One of my toughest critics on the school board (and a person

EXHIBIT 8.2 **Superintendent self-evaluation**

Self-Evaluation—September, 2011

I believe I am fluent in my understanding of various aspects of educational leadership, and I look for every opportunity to improve my knowledge base. I am well-versed on topics related to curriculum, instruction, and assessment, and this area of responsibility is the one about which I care most. This summer, I attended a three-week executive leadership program at the Harvard Kennedy School that focused on topics, such as: data analysis, negotiations, religion, political issues, leadership, finance, and more. This provided me with an opportunity to fine-tune my educational leadership skills.

Despite my background and interest, I need to give instructional leadership more time and attention. While making surface-level changes is relatively easy (e.g., this past year, I worked with administrators to complete a curriculum revision process that is practical, tied to our strategic plan, and aimed at continuous improvement), what has been much harder to do is to find ways to impact the instructional core. The reason this is difficult is because the changes that need to happen are at the classroom level and require systems, structures, and the human resources needed to help teachers find new instructional strategies when they see a need to change or those they have been using are no longer effective.

In urban schools, this work tends to get accomplished in a "leadership by memo" approach. Administrators regularly distribute bulletins addressing this instructional misstep or that classroom expectation. My experience as a teacher tells me that the single most important way to change one's practice is to involve that person directly in the process of identifying the changes that are needed. In other words, don't send a teacher a copy of the curriculum frameworks and expect changes to happen miraculously; instead, engage teachers in thoughtful and respectful conversations about how their students are performing and work with them to experiment with different approaches and ways to improve.

As I put into writing what needs to occur, it sounds easy enough. So why didn't this happen during the past year? I believe it is fair to say that this type of systemic change tends to be harder to do in a larger system; consequently, the improvements happen slowly. It is also the case that the right staffing model may not be in place to advance this work. Two years ago, we established an organizational chart to ensure proper oversight; it appears that we may not have the staff in place to advance the agenda that could lead to the greatest gains in student achievement. The current structure involves oversight by the Assistant Superintendent, and the person in this position is expected to oversee teaching and learning at the elementary levels with help from consultants and principals, attending to all other aspects of the job, including oversight at the secondary level. Those who supervise in various content areas at the secondary level also teach classes, as they supervise teaching and learning for students in middle and high school.

The idea behind this organizational model was to enlist the help of consultants in various elementary initiatives that required a certain level of expertise. For example, as we focused on writing, the Assistant Superintendent enlisted the expertise of a writing specialist. This idea was appealing because it meant that we were more focused and far less inclined to have multiple initiatives happening at once. However, while this works on paper, it does not necessarily work in practice. In the future, it may be wise to explore a model that includes a Director of Elementary Instruction. In addition, it may also be wise to consider restructuring the Assistant Superintendent's position to more closely align with the responsibilities associated with a Director of Secondary Instruction whose primary focus is (1) student achievement; and (2) oversight and responsibility for the curriculum supervisors at the secondary level. The addition of literacy and mathematics coaches at the elementary level could also provide much needed support.

In practical terms, due to the economic environment, the addition of administrative staff is unlikely any time soon. Staffing needs aside, there are administrative structures in place and better ways that we can organize using the resources that exist. Upon further reflection, putting together a random task force here and there last year was my approach, but it was "hit or miss" and it was difficult to make improvements at all schools, and in all classrooms. With the exception of the district writing assessment created in grade 3 this past year, I did not have the structures in place to organize in a systematic way and make the lasting improvements that we would like to see. I have given this topic much thought, and I have exciting ideas about how to get this work done, which I will include when I present recommendations for district goals.

whom I admire greatly because he was always truthful and kept me grounded) stated publicly during a televised meeting that this was one of the most honest self-assessments he had ever seen. He said he was impressed with my performance and in agreement with the areas that I identified as needing improvement. This is the same school board member who cast the sole vote *against* my appointment as superintendent of schools but later acknowledged publicly that he was pleasantly surprised that his initial assessment of me was wrong, and I was the right person for the job after all. After discussing this self-evaluation, my school board evaluated me in open session, and they rated my performance as "Meeting" or "Exceeding" the standards in all categories. The outcome may have been different if I had pretended everything was perfect because it would have sent a signal to my school board that I am oblivious to the improvements that I need to make as a leader and the work that needs to happen in the school system.

Effective communication builds trust, and it takes more than good public speaking, listening, and nonverbal skills to establish productive superintendent–school board relationships. When you use sophisticated communication approaches with your school board, it reinforces your belief in collaboration and your respect for the board's countless contributions to your schools and students. Communication must be honest, timely, and differentiated, taking into account your school board members' preferences to build stronger bonds. As superintendent, you must be willing to speak out and speak up, working to advocate for your board and confronting the inevitable challenges that arise when people with differences work together in any setting. If you practice these advanced communication techniques consistently, you will build a high-functioning superintendent–school board team.

TAUNTON PUBLIC SCHOOLS

Dr. Julie Hackett,
Superintendent of Schools

215 Harris Street
Taunton, Massachusetts 02780
Tel. (508) 821-1100
Fax (508) 821-1177

Academic excellence for every student, in every classroom, in every school.

September 1, 2012

Dear Commissioner:

At a meeting held on August 15, 2012, members of the Taunton School Committee expressed their disenchantment with the number of State initiatives currently in the implementation phase. They unanimously passed a motion to invite a representative of the Department of Elementary and Secondary Education (ESE) to a Committee of the Whole meeting to discuss the various State initiatives and associated impacts, such as time, training, resources, and time on learning. On behalf of the Taunton School Committee, I am writing to request that either you or a member of the ESE meet with the Taunton School Committee at a date and time that is convenient to address three major issues: unfunded mandates, the impacts of over-testing, and the impossibility of effective implementation.

Two years ago, the Committee asked me to send you a communication to express their displeasure with the move from the Massachusetts Curriculum Frameworks to the Common Core which appeared to be driven by the State's interest in Race to the Top. The Committee reasoned that Massachusetts already had high standards, and in comparison to other states, we were performing well on several measures, including the National Assessment of Educational Progress (NAEP), so why would we want to make changes just to chase dollars? Their primary concern was that this level of involvement could spread and interfere with other areas of education.

The Taunton School Committee now believes that their fears were well-founded. They observe that we are in the process of implementing a dizzying array of initiatives that will overburden districts financially and, worse yet, cause harm to children who are the unwitting victims of over-testing. Last year at Taunton High School, which services students in grades 8–12, over 3,600 tests were administered. This includes 400 retests, at least 1,400 tenth grade/high school science tests, and over 1,800 eighth grade tests. This resulted in a substantial financial cost to the school system to pay educators the contractual rate required when a planning period is taken away in order for them to proctor the exams—but it was our students who paid the highest price in terms of instructional time lost.

In the 2011–2012 school year, the high school had 25 full days of testing and 10–12 days of make-up testing. Each of these more than 35 days of testing took significant time away from students, teachers, administrators and support staff. Each test represents at least three hours of teaching time lost (not accounting for the large number of students who take extra time on one or more of the testing days), for a total of over 10,800 hours. To put this into perspective, this is the

The Taunton Public School System does not discriminate on the basis of age, color, sex, religion, national origin, sexual orientation or disability.

equivalent of over 1,660 individual absences, or nearly eight students not attending school for the entire year, and this is only for the Massachusetts Comprehensive Assessment System (MCAS), one battery of State tests. It is reasonable to believe that the 10,800 hours of lost instructional time could easily be doubled when one considers that test fatigue is a major factor that affects time on learning. Most educators will tell you that a student who sits for a two- to three-hour test is not as eager or ready to learn as he/she might be on a non-testing day. When taken together, instructional time lost due to MCAS testing at Taunton High School is closer to 20,000 instructional hours. While accountability is important, too much testing has hampered our students' ability to be critical thinkers who are intellectually curious and joyful learners, and we worry about what the future holds.

Now, with its new initiatives, the ESE plans to add more assessments to the mix, which is of great concern to the Taunton School Committee. At their request, I constructed an "initiatives matrix," which I have included for your information along with a cost analysis of each initiative. The purpose of this exercise was to keep track of the various initiatives and the financial impacts, to better understand the implications of each one, and to monitor the associated timelines. It should be noted that the data gathered in this document were not easily accessible, which leads one to wonder whether the ESE has conducted such an exercise of its own.

The list of initiatives currently in the implementation stage includes: the transition of the Massachusetts Curriculum Frameworks to the Common Core State Standards (CCSS); the Educator Evaluation System (EES); Partnership of Assessment for Readiness of College and Careers (PARCC); Rethinking Equity and Teaching for English Language Learners (RETELL); World Class Instructional Design and Assessment (WIDA); Assessing Comprehension and Communication in English State-to-State (ACCESS)—but the list does not stop there.

In addition to conducting a cost analysis of each initiative, I have also been asked to point out that for any given initiative there is a subset of initiatives that is hidden from plain view and not immediately obvious. For example, the transition from the MA Curriculum Frameworks to the Common Core Curriculum Standards (CCCS) is not as simple as an exercise of realignment. The implications are far-reaching, and the demands are significant both in terms of time and financial resources. Here are but a few of the considerations that we must make to adequately address this one initiative alone:

- Provide foundational professional development to help educators understand the shift from the MA Curriculum Frameworks to the CCSS
- Examine CCSS and realign the curricula in the core area by grade level
- Purchase new textbooks and materials to align with the CCSS
- Provide high-quality, ongoing professional development for the purchase of a new program or materials
- Upgrade technology infrastructure, hardware, and software to utilize the digital components of the program, including online tools, assessments, and resources
- Repeat this entire process for each content area

So far, Taunton has only scratched the surface of our transition to the Common Core, and it is not for lack of trying. Last year after a pilot and a thoughtful process, we purchased a reading series for PK-6 that is aligned to the Common Core. Due to a carefully planned approach, teachers and administrators are excited about the new reading series, and we have begun professional development in this area. Workshops to assist teachers and administrators in the implementation of the new reading program were held this summer, and related costs involved compensation for the professional development providers and payment for teachers at their contractual hourly rate. Time and money being what they are, we also utilized the first day back to school to provide additional training, which is not ideal. By the time we are fully implemented, the cost of the new reading program and the necessary professional development for PK-6 will be upwards of $500,000, not including technology costs. For an adequate transition from the MA Curriculum Frameworks to the CCSS, when each content area is considered, the associated expenditures are conservatively in the millions of dollars for a school system our size.

And that price tag is the cost for just one of the six State initiatives mentioned. The same exercise can be played out with the Educator Evaluation System (EES), another State initiative driven by Race to the Top. Here is an abbreviated list of what it will take to adequately implement the Educator Evaluation System (EES):

- Provide foundational professional development to help educators understand the purpose and components of the EES
- Provide professional development on evaluation rubrics and associated consequences
- Provide professional development to help educators write goals that are meaningful and measurable
- Provide professional development on understanding formative and summative assessments
- Work with principals to develop manageable systems for completing the evaluations
- Develop multiple measures or a comprehensive local assessment system to ensure objective and fair evaluations for all, including: administrators, nurses, guidance counselors, and educators in every content area (e.g., English/Language Arts, Mathematics, Science, Social Studies, Visual Arts, Performing Arts, Physical Education, Health/Wellness, Career Technical Education, Foreign Languages, etc.)
- Provide professional development to educators to teach them about collaborative goal setting in grade level teams, how to monitor progress, how to collect evidence, and so on
- Provide time for educators to develop thoughtful goals both individually and in teams
- Provide professional development to educators to gain input on the comprehensive assessment system and to help educators understand each assessment being used, why it is important, and what it will tell us about our students' achievement
- Purchase a student information system powerful enough to enable us to store and explore the comprehensive local assessment data to make appropriate determinations about the success of students, teachers, other educators, and principals
- Upgrade technology infrastructure, hardware and software in order to have access to assessments and other materials associated with the EES
- Provide ongoing high-quality professional development to modify and refine the comprehensive local assessment system

The importance of cohesion was underscored in the ESE's presentation of the new Educator Evaluation System, yet a cohesive strategy appears to be lacking with respect to the ESE's implementation of its various initiatives. While the ESE's focus on improving teaching and learning is commendable, and any one of the ESE's six initiatives holds merit, it is unrealistic to pretend that there is enough time in the day to adequately implement these initiatives simultaneously. It has been said that "to do two things at once is to do neither," which may be the unintended consequence of the hasty implementation of so many initiatives all at once. The great irony is that in the end, too many distractions caused by so many initiatives aimed at improving teaching and learning will ultimately diminish all that we hoped to accomplish for the children in Massachusetts.

On behalf of the Taunton School Committee and the children whom we serve, thank you for taking the time to listen to our concerns. The Committee eagerly awaits your response to their invitation to attend an upcoming Committee of the Whole meeting.

Sincerely,

Julie Hackett

Julie Hackett, Ed.D.
Superintendent of Schools
Taunton Public Schools

CHAPTER NINE

Time to Change Your Relationship Status

If moral purpose is job one, then relationships are job two, as you can't get anywhere without them.

—MICHAEL FULLAN, 2001

IT'S COMPLICATED

It's complicated, but it doesn't have to be. If you are a social media technophobe like me, you might not know that Facebook users have the option of posting their relationship status online for the world to see. The tech-savvy can select from various posts ranging from "single" to "in a relationship" or (for those who want to add a little mystery and intrigue) "it's complicated," which apparently hints at an impending breakup or dissatisfaction in the relationship.[1] Superintendent and school board relationships may be complex, but they do not have to be complicated. When you adopt the right mindset, you can take on the most challenging educational reforms and at the same time create highly effective school board relationships to help your students achieve more.

Now that you have made your way through this book, it is my hope that you are ready to announce your new superintendent–school board relationship status to the world. While teaching and learning are at the core of your work

> A CYCLE OF CONTINUOUS IMPROVEMENT: REVIEW, REFLECT, RENEW
>
> 1. Superintendent and school board self-assessments
> 2. Biannual retreats
> 3. Annual conference
> 4. Celebrations of success

today, relationship building is at the heart of it, and vibrant school cultures are the result of close connections between you and your school board. The strategies throughout the chapters in this book were designed to usher in a new way of thinking to help you, if you are a reform-minded superintendent, to view your responsibility and relationship with school boards differently. Superintendent and school board connections are as complex and challenging as any, and getting these connections on track requires a considerable amount of your time and attention. If you adopt a realistic approach and have the wherewithal to know that you can overcome the inevitable school board challenges, the long-term gains (not to mention the headaches and heartaches that you will be spared) will make the effort worthwhile.

What mindset is needed, then, for an overburdened superintendent to make such a long-term commitment to relationship building? Effective superintendent–school board relationships require your steadfast devotion and perseverance, which is similar in many ways to the approach that we take with our own families, whom we may not always like but to whom most are always loyal. As in familial relationships, nearly all superintendents and school boards experience conflict of some sort, and every so often even the best among us gets into a spat with a son, daughter, brother, sister, partner, spouse, mother, or father. Sometimes these controversies are inconsequential, and at other times they are quite serious. No matter how upsetting or egregious, however, few among us rarely ever give up and stop trying to find ways to improve or repair a relationship with a family member.

This same level of compassion and commitment is needed in public education today, yet superintendents and school boards wash their hands of one another all the time. This is especially true for the "rock star" reformers who consider themselves change agents hired to blast their way through initiatives ostensibly in the best interests of the students. Yet, even if an initiative is better for students in the short term, what good does it do if the changes last only as long as the leader? Should sustainability of these educational reforms be a factor in whether or not they are deemed a success? Schools will be better when superintendents and school leaders consistently demonstrate the same level of patience, care, and persistence in their school board relationships that most do in their personal ones. When school leaders set aside their egos, adopt an "all in" mindset, and treat their school board relationships like they do their familial ones, superintendent–school board dynamics will vastly improve, and so too will public education.

THIS IS THE BUSINESS WE HAVE CHOSEN

Superintendents and school leaders are faced with an enormous set of responsibilities, and it may seem impossible to add to an ever-increasing list of difficult-to-manage expectations. On any given day, you are likely to encounter the individual agendas of up to eight or more different school board members in addition to the wants and needs of the collective body—a job in and of itself. School board members' issues run the gamut, and the onslaught of concerns may look something like this: one member is worried about a neighbor's child who is struggling in school and needs tutoring, another wants to discuss the new state fingerprinting law right away, one needs just a few minutes of your time to talk about the possible employment of a friend, another wants answers for his constituents who are demanding to know when repairs will be made to the baseball field, one thinks it would be a good idea to talk soon about the city's financial challenges and the potential impact on the school department, another is hurt and upset that you didn't return his call right away, someone else wants to discuss recent state and federal nutrition guidelines and ways to counteract the harmful effect of these policy decisions, and yet another is going through an extremely painful personal situation and could use a friendly check-in from you.

As superintendent of schools, you know full well you have a lot to do, and your school board members' issues represent only a fraction of the work you must accomplish. You know that the job of a superintendent is rife with challenges, but, then again, what educator's job isn't these days? School leaders need to practice the same "no excuses" advice we so often find ourselves giving to educators when our teachers tell us how difficult it is to get every child to meet or exceed a standard or graduate on time. In this era of accountability, more and more school leaders are committed to helping all children reach their potential, and they have little tolerance for teachers and administrators who claim it an impossibility to achieve this goal given the many societal issues impacting public education. Frustrated educators point out that our children come from impoverished backgrounds, their families do not seem to care, and students cannot always do this demanding work when they are suffering unspeakable traumas. Optimistic superintendents like me know that students can achieve more than we ever thought possible when educators allow themselves to believe it.

But superintendents like me also need to exercise caution and take care to practice what we preach. We cannot make excuses that it is too hard to do the relationship-building work with our school board because this member is uncaring, that member has a personal agenda, or this one is out to get me. There is a great scene in Francis Ford Coppola's *The Godfather, Part II,* in which Michael Corleone questions Hyman Roth about a death, and Roth responds irreverently that how he died is immaterial because "this is the business we have chosen." Perhaps not the most uplifting analogy for a school leader, but it is a mantra that superintendents could use today. This *is* the business we have chosen, and when we signed that contract and made that commitment to that school district to make a difference for that student body, we knew there would be nothing easy about it.

This may be the business we have chosen, but by no stretch of the imagination am I suggesting that you should act on demand and do everything that every school board member asks of you, particularly when you are faced with an unreasonable request or a demand that may derail important district priorities. If you pander to school board members' needs, you may quickly lose focus and put yourself at risk of an emotional breakdown or an early burnout. It is important to be prepared for the time when school board members will ask you to do something that you believe compromises your values and threatens to disrupt the important work that you are trying to accomplish on behalf of your students. I am not suggesting this because school board members are malicious or you are always right; it is simply a function of working with people who have different points of view and values. Finding ways to reach agreement and satisfy all parties is important, but as you saw in chapter 8, finding tactful ways to say no while maintaining a strong, healthy relationship with your school board is critical.

Consequently, you must be able to distinguish between school board desires that *may* or *may not* need to be addressed and those school board needs that *must* be addressed. A few years ago I was in the process of contacting each school board member to explain why I was appointing a particular person to the job, and I invited members to come see me individually if they wanted to further discuss the matter. This situation rankled one of my school board members who (unlike most others) fervently believed that superintendents should be left alone to do their jobs without school board interference. This particular board member did not hide his exasperation when he learned that I was checking in with him and all his colleagues on a pending appointment, intending to offer them an opportunity for further discussion. His response was, "You're going to meet with every person on this? Wouldn't it be nice if they would leave you alone and let you focus on the job you were hired to do for a change?"

In Massachusetts, the Education Reform Act of 1993 changed the hiring practices of school systems, and the responsibility for hiring and firing was shifted from school boards to superintendents. In this particular school board member's view, the superintendent had the authority to make the appointment under the law, so that should have been the end of the discussion. While the board member was technically correct, I knew that the person I intended to hire was not the candidate that some members had wanted in the position, which might cause hard feelings. You may well have the authority to act in a certain manner, but if you elect to exercise this authority at all times and without discussion, you are certain to compromise your relationship with board members and waste a great deal more time doing damage control than necessary. Being angry with you is much harder when school board members or the public know the thinking behind a controversial decision being made.

Through the years I have learned that I would rather spend my time working to improve my relationship with my school board than waste my time lamenting the fact that my job as schools' chief would be easier without them. As I explained to my school board member, *this is the business I have chosen,* and I believe strongly that getting everyone on board *is* the work of the superintendency. As a school leader, I wholeheartedly believe that, as Blaydes says, "one's philosophy is not best expressed in words; it is expressed in the choices one makes . . . and the choices we make are ultimately our responsibility."[2] The choice I have made as a leader is to attend to the needs of all of my school board members when it matters most in order to help my educators and students progress. My school board is my second family, and the attitudes that we adopt make a difference in our ability to work successfully together so we can give all of our students a fighting chance.

A CYCLE OF CONTINUOUS REVIEW, REFLECTION, AND RENEWAL

Despite their mutual admiration, children and parents get frustrated with each other from time to time, and believe it or not, so do superintendents and school boards. When an even greater challenge threatens to derail the relationship, the situation can be hard on all involved and particularly tough on a superintendent's ego. Most school leaders engaged in this work care deeply about education and believe that their approach is right, just, and in the best interests of the students they serve; otherwise, they would not be taking these steps. Superintendents I know say that the work is so deeply personal that a confrontation with a school board member can feel like a question of their integrity or an assault on their character. A former school board member used to joke that she earns "slightly less than five cents an hour" for doing the job. If you think it is hard to have your intentions questioned, imagine how it feels to be a public servant who invests her own time and effort into a job—for which there is little or no compensation or glory—only to have her motives questioned by a superintendent.

Relationships between even the most conscientious superintendents and school boards can get sidetracked from time to time, and the wise school leader anticipates and plans for this inevitability. You may do everything right; you may forge strong connections with your school board members through the entry and strategic planning process, you may establish an agreed-upon set of norms and beliefs, and you may include your school board and school community in inclusive goal setting, using the community input process to tackle significant educational reforms to achieve your goals. Similar to curriculum guides that have a way of ending up on classroom shelves, all this relationship-building work is for naught if it is inconsistently practiced, reviewed, and revised.

Once you have made an effort to establish positive and productive relationships with your school board, your work is far from over. A cycle of continuous review, reflection, and renewal helps to maintain the positive relationships that you and the school board worked so hard to build throughout the year. I regularly use four important strategies to ensure that my school board and I are working to continuously improve our superintendent–school board relationships, including (1) superintendent and school board self-assessments, (2) biannual retreats, (3) annual conference, and (4) celebrations of success.

Superintendent and School Board Self-Assessments

There are many ways to hold yourself accountable, but what works best for me is to have relationship-building expectations embedded in the superintendent's evaluation tool. A few years ago, my school board was in the process of revising the superintendent's evaluation policy and rubric, and I offered to collect samples of evaluation rubrics and tools that might hold promise. For obvious reasons, I intentionally selected evaluation tools and rubrics that included performance indicators designed to measure a superintendent's ability to establish effective school board relationships. In the current superintendent's evaluation tool used by my school board, there are six areas of responsibility, and "Responsibility #1" is "Relationship with the School Committee," which includes the following five performance indicators: (1) keeps the school committee informed on the issues, needs, and operation of the school system; (2) gives a recommendation to the school committee on items requiring action based on thorough research and analysis; (3) interprets, supports, and executes the intent of school committee policy; (4) seeks and maintains a professional working relationship with the school committee; and (5) supports and enhances the school committee's core values, budget commitments, and budget priorities.

An effective way for you to hold yourself accountable is to ask the school board to include such a standard and performance indicators in school board policy and in your evaluation tool. It is useful to identify areas that could give rise to problematic situations unique to your district that may strain the superintendent–school board relationship. For example, due to conflicts in the past between superintendents and school board members in my school system, it would be unlikely for any superintendent to survive the job without "supporting and enhancing the school committee's core values" (Performance Indicator #5). Using the strategies discussed in this book, you will be better equipped to identify these unspoken expectations and make them explicit. You are more likely to put effort and energy into that which is measured, and if relationship building is missing from your evaluation tool, you may not give this strategy the attention it deserves. Failing to address this issue may not only compromise your employment but, as you have seen, also could have harmful consequences for the school district and your students.

Each year I submit a written self-evaluation on my progress toward these standards and my goals; this is an effective way to ensure that I spend time reviewing my efforts to build stronger relationships with the school board. As I review my progress through the year and opportunities for growth, I consider ways that I could get better at building stronger relationships with my school board, and I build these methods into my future goals and efforts in the following year. It is useful for you to structure similar opportunities for the school board to review their progress individually and as a group. When I first began working with my school board on their own self-assessments, they performed the assessments in a group because that approach was less threatening.

You are a teacher in this relationship-building work with your school board, and that means you must be willing to model what it is you want for the system. I want members of my team to take risks and have enough trust and confidence in themselves to admit that there is always room for improvement. I try to encourage this thinking by publicly taking responsibility when I am wrong about something—which you might be surprised to learn has happened on more than one occasion. As time passed in my work with the school board, we were able to evaluate ourselves—not just how we functioned as a group—and these self-assessments helped us have a more open and honest discussion about how each of us approached the work and how we wanted to improve. I knew we hit pay dirt when I heard one school board member say to her colleagues, "I really need to get better at this," and the culture of mutual respect and trust that we have worked so hard to build continues to evolve.

In appendix 3.2, I included a self-assessment checklist that individual school board members can use and discuss with their colleagues. It may be helpful for you to provide time during a retreat to complete the self-assessment and then model for your school board how you view your own successes and challenges. I then suggest a "turn and talk" exercise in which you have school board members discuss with a partner those aspects of the self-assessment that they want to report, and then those who are willing can share in a whole group discussion. In appendix 3.8, I included an agenda that I used with the school board outlining a group-assessment process. Taking this approach is useful when you are first beginning to establish better relationship-building dynamics with your school board.

Biannual Retreats

Another good way to systematize opportunities for reflection is to prearrange biannual retreats that are focused on strengthening relationships between you and your school board. A word of caution: if not carefully planned, retreats can quickly devolve into work sessions in which you are establishing the school board calendar or reviewing policy. Complete those types of activities in a subcommittee meeting, when you can, and make your retreats a singular experience in which you focus exclusively on relationship building. It is helpful to work with your school board to identify a time when you will reflect on your progress halfway through the year (January or February) and again at the end of the year (July or August). Life is busy, and relationship building can be uncomfortable for some, so find ways to memorialize your agreement to retreat and focus on relationship building once or twice a year. You can embed your agreement in your norms and beliefs protocol, or you can embed it in school board policy. The point is to make certain that nothing will get in the way of this important work.

I meet with my school board twice a year (typically in January and July), and we try to do so off-site. Our locations have changed through the years, but we have had retreats in a school; at Gillette Stadium in Foxboro, Massachusetts; in restaurants; at the home of a school board member; and most recently at a school board member's seaside cottage. If you are able to do so, meeting off-site is important because it signals that relationship building is the primary focus and the purpose of the meeting is different than others. Our early retreats were on-site in a teacher's room (instead of our typical meeting place) due to the initial reluctance of some school board members to hold meetings off-site. Our school board meetings are televised, so holding meetings off-site is a good way for us to get away from the cameras. It could be difficult to get anyone to open up on camera, and in order for retreats to be effective, you and school board members need to feel safe.

Our best retreats are the ones that have been off-site, and whenever possible, I highly recommend a change in venue. We choose to post the retreats as we would a regular school board meeting because our retreats always include an agenda, and the idea of meeting without posting was unsettling to some school board members due to transparency laws. Posting the meeting put school board members at ease, and they now take an active role in determining the location for the retreat and the content and issues that need to be discussed. We recently held our tenth retreat, and we spent some time reflecting on our first retreat together. At that retreat, there was awkwardness and tension as we tried to work through various relational challenges that certain members took quite personally. At our tenth retreat, the school board members and I took pride in the caliber of the conversation and how far we have come in our ability to problem-solve and work through difficult issues together.

Annual Conference

Another important way that I work to continuously improve superintendent–school board relationships is to attend a conference with my board members each year. In Massachusetts we are fortunate to have an annual conference every November, beginning on the day after elections, that is cosponsored by our state's superintendent and school board associations. Presentations are made by superintendents and school board members individually and collectively, and they share useful information about relevant school topics. Each year for the past six years, my entire school board and I have attended the conference for at least one day together, and sometimes more. There is a special dinner and guest speaker on a certain night, and we make it a point to participate on this day and evening. While other superintendents and school boards attend, they do not always spend time together, which is a missed opportunity. My school board takes a great deal of pride in being together as a team, and we typically walk away from these sessions feeling good about our work together and inspired to do more.

Celebrations of Success

There is no better way for you and your school board members to experience renewal than to celebrate your collective successes. I know superintendents who believe it is their responsibility to identify the school system's flaws. They worry that the school board and the school community will rest on their laurels and become complacent without a wake-up call that shows them there is an imperative to improve. Very often their speeches, written communication, and public conversations are aimed at problem identification. In my view, they are right in their thinking, but wrong in their approach. Exceptional leaders should have the capacity to see into the future and envision how their schools could look, and they also need to possess the skills to move the school community toward this ideal. Educators and school boards need to be inspired to do the challenging and difficult work that is ahead of them. It is human nature for us to run in the other direction if someone tells us we are terrible at a certain thing. Superintendents must confront pervasive issues to improve schools, but it is all in the approach. A relationship-building strategy I use is to talk about the successes in the system whenever possible, giving the school board credit for their role in it. I share good stories about the school board's role in the district's successes when I present my budget to the city council, in newsletters, and during the School Community

Recognition events that we hold three times a year. Each year I also include a list of district successes in my self-evaluation (see appendix 9.1), highlighting our accomplishments in my opening day remarks each year, making sure to point out the school board's role in them.

BUT DON'T JUST TAKE MY WORD FOR IT

Any superintendent who writes a book on the secrets to successful leadership has poetic license to tell you that her ideas worked. My hope is that this book moves you, changing the way you approach and think about the school reform work that you do with your school board. If you are a superintendent who considers relationship building too "touchy feely," and you are skeptical of putting this extra effort into building a productive team, the best way I know how to compel you to give it a try is to hear the thoughts of the school board members themselves. One of my board members who lived through the "Yes, heil Hitler, sieg heil" days was a skeptic at first, but as you will read in the afterword, she became a believer, and she had this to say about our superintendent–school board relationship transformation: "We are ordinary people who developed an extraordinary commitment to make it better. We did it by trusting each other, educating ourselves about the needs in the community, and by respecting each other."

This extraordinary commitment to improving your students' lives is also within your reach—you just have to want it. It was Lao Tzu, a great philosopher and poet of ancient China and a contemporary of Confucius who lived in 6 B.C.,[3] who said:

> Go to the people. Learn from them. Start with what they know. Build with what they have. The best leaders when the job is done, when the task is accomplished, the people will say we have done it ourselves.

It is my hope that this book has inspired you to go to your school board, learn from them, and start with what they know. Listen closely to their needs and teach them how you can do the work better together. Problem-solve, collaborate, and make the time to openly discuss the tensions that exist, never forgetting to celebrate your accomplishments. When superintendents and school boards work together, children grow academically, socially, and emotionally, becoming the beneficiaries of your long-lasting, sustainable school reforms. The children you serve deserve nothing less than a world-class education, and a superintendent and school board united by a singular focus and purpose—the success of every student.

TPS Achievements and Highlights, 2012-2013

Thanks to the support of the Taunton School Committee and the significant efforts of our extraordinary school community, there is much to celebrate. Our recent accomplishments include:

- **Advocacy—**Several letters written to State officials concerning Chapter 74 matters, high stakes testing, and the implementation and cost of various initiatives.
- **BSRI Implementation**—All seven elementary schools now have their own Taunton Literacy Coach and work directly with a BSRI Principal Coach and a BSRI Literacy Coach.
- **Caleb Barnum School to the Edward F. Leddy** - Relocated Barnum students to Leddy, creating a safer, ADA-accessible facility with a new playground.
- **Capital Improvements—**Renovation of the Robert H. Park Auditorium seats at Taunton High School; new permanent structure for the Tiger Tent Café; plans for new tennis courts in progress (to be located on Williams Street for community use).
- **Chapter 74—**Three new programs approved this year for a total of five Ch. 74 programs; additional Chapter 70 revenue in the past few years totals approximately $2 million.
- **Contract Negotiations**—Successfully negotiated six contracts and engaged in extensive collective bargaining on other important matters (educator evaluation, inclusion, Taunton Alternative High School staffing, etc.).
- **Donald D. Johnson Operations and Efficiencies Award Winner, 2012—**Only school system in Massachusetts to earn this distinction; previous winners are Belmont and Lexington.
- **Dropout Rate**—Enlisted all administrators and reduced the TPS Dropout Rate from 5.5% to 4.4%, one of the lowest rates in the history of our school system. The new data will be released in January, and we expect that rate to be significantly lower at that time.
- **Inclusion**—Finalized one of the first districtwide inclusion agreements in the Commonwealth. Expanded the number of inclusion teachers from 22 to 48, significantly improving the student/staff ratio from 1:17 to 1:4; increased the number of high school inclusion classrooms from 6 to 22. Graduate-level inclusion course and certification process for 130+ education assistants.
- **Leadership Team**—Restructured positions, recruited, and appointed a highly effective Leadership Team with three new members: Assistant Superintendent for Curriculum and Instruction; Director of Transportation and Student Services; and Legal Counsel for Pupil and Personnel at no additional cost to the school system.
- **Taunton "Early College" Alternative High School**—Successfully planned, staffed, and opened a new TAHS. Secured more than $200K in competitive grant funds to support the efforts; formed a unique partnership with Bristol Community College to offer free dual enrollment courses to students; and graduated 68 TAHS at-risk students in our first year.

Afterword

EARLY WORK WITH THE SCHOOL BOARD

When I think back to my early days on the school board, I remember that it was crazy. It was very hard to understand the impact of everything because some people were good at masking the consequences of a vote, there was no place for an opinion, and there were alliances. It was hard to navigate the jungle and get to a point of understanding with the superintendent or school board members—or even to disagree. As a member of the public, I remember being enraged that there was such a "disconnect" from the behavior that we expected of the students and staff in the district and how school board members were acting in meetings. There was no understanding of what was happening in the schools, and even a sense of bullying. I had to gird myself as if I was having to prepare for a battle, and it felt as though I had walked into this artificially intense situation on red alert. It was kind of like a seven-second radio censorship lapse before someone said something because I knew I would be dealing with a headline the next day, hanging out there all by myself on a limb. There was absolute discomfort and fear, and I always felt at risk.

What do I remember about the tough times? It was like a bad marriage. I remember my son used to say, "I don't know how you can do your hair, put on your make-up, pick out an outfit, and go someplace where people are going to yell at you." Most of us didn't say anything—there was a knee-jerk behavior. Certain individuals knew what buttons to push. It was petty and vindictive, and I was so horrified by the bad behavior of the former superintendent and school board members. I couldn't believe this eighth grade behavior was taking place on the actual, televised meetings at the highest levels in the city. The students laughed it off, I think, and there were a lot of headshakes from the staff. The relationship back then was mean-spirited. There was this personal tension, but it wasn't necessarily overt. I remember the meetings would run until 1 a.m., and I didn't know any better—I thought that's how long they were supposed to run. It's up to the superintendent to help manage that, but as a new school board member, I didn't really understand the role of the superintendent as the chief executive or CEO. Obviously, it was embarrassing; I was a little bit ashamed to be involved with a school board that was characterized by bad manners and unprofessionalism.

HOW THE SUPERINTENDENT–SCHOOL BOARD RELATIONSHIP-BUILDING WORK MADE A DIFFERENCE

Our relationship-building work *did* work; it was respectable, and I wasn't embarrassed any more to say I was serving on the school board. We learned over time that this was a business meeting, and it was not a time to explore, expose, and dazzle the public with dedication and diligence. School board meetings should be where decisions are made; they are the "in-the-open" product or conclusion—not the process. The accessibility of the superintendent is so important in this. If I have concerns, I know that the superintendent is my source. If we are trying to solve a problem, I have to give you time to explain why your vision is the right one, and that means spending time with you to ask questions and learn more about what you are thinking. In our work together, I know that I am entitled to disagree and to pick and choose what I believe is right. On camera, I can say, "These were my concerns, these were the answers to the questions that I asked, and this is what I think." I might agree with the superintendent or not, and if I don't, I know that I can say, "These are still my concerns." I learned that a good superintendent will work to address my concerns or help me understand why they can't be addressed.

After not renewing the former superintendent's contract, we started working together on the relationship-building strategies, and there was such a difference. For once, everybody was facing the same way in the canoe. I remember our first retreat. It was the first time we had socialized off-site, and that really made a difference. I remember when a school board member (a former tax assessor) broke the ice and said, "Well, it's very nice to be here at your grossly under-assessed home." We all laughed together and relaxed. It was a huge step forward in changing the culture of the school board–superintendent dynamic. It was important for us to get to know each other in a different way. When there was a conflict or a problem, consensus was reached more quickly than ever before. It had nothing to do with giving up beliefs . . . We were all beginning to look at things differently, and we were able to get to the heart of the matter without taking it personally. I also loved having those community input team meetings with parents about things like Honors. What was wonderful was to not be campaigning, but to be really educating the public about our ideas. We were able to go from table to table and sit with the public and build mini-relationships when parents would come in and be skeptical at first. Through the power of my own belief, I was able to convince them that there was a better way and say, "Just hold my hand, and this will be fine." I felt like I was able to make a difference.

LESSONS FROM THE SUPERINTENDENT–SCHOOL BOARD RELATIONSHIP-BUILDING PROCESS

A good superintendent is like an effective teacher. Just like a teacher, you have to deal with who's thrown at you. Superintendents who leave out school board members are as ineffective as teachers who exclude students in the classroom. It's easy teaching like that—in an exclusionary way. It's easy to bring tablets down from the Mount and say, "This is how it must be done." Any teacher can get people to believe in what she wants them to; it just takes time. I could say,

"Romeo and Juliet behaved impetuously, and that's why they died. Next?" It's much, much harder for me to set up situations and guide those in class to the conclusion desired, and that's true for superintendents, too. It's a slow process at first, but eventually the kids—and the school board members—internalize the habit of cooperation and dialoguing to reach a consensus. As superintendent, you have to work at it and make an effort with your school board if they want to make a difference.

I also learned that there can be challenges and disagreements, and we can still have strong relationships. I remember when we dealt with the school closings and consolidations. It was the hardest time for us, but it was also a time when we felt like a unit—we were all contributing, and there was a sense of bravery and respect. I made a different choice than my colleagues on an important vote, but I was never abused by seven others for having a different opinion. The norms and beliefs gave me and others the mindset and focus that when the vote is taken, it's over. I'm big on what's fair; we need to fight the good fight, and when it's done, it's done. How we approached our work together and things like the norms and beliefs reminded us of the importance of our own good manners and being brought up in a time when the way you treated others mattered. In the end we learned to present an opinion, dialogue, reach consensus, and accept things with good grace and move on.

IMPACT OF THE SUPERINTENDENT–SCHOOL BOARD RELATIONSHIP BUILDING ON THE SCHOOL COMMUNITY AND STUDENTS

The school board and superintendent took on the aura of a professional, unified, educationally focused entity. We (all nine of us) became respectable and respected. This effort reestablished us all as a valuable unit, focused on doing what we were elected to do: make the hard decisions necessary to improve our kids' opportunities. I had maintained my strong friendships with many teachers still in the classroom, and these friends—and other staff members who were really just acquaintances—made it a point to say how wonderful it was to not be embarrassed anymore by the antics of the school board and the administration. They felt that the school board and superintendent had a *real* focus on education, improving the perception of our entire school system, and encouraging and promoting the achievements of all.

ADVICE FOR SKEPTICAL SUPERINTENDENTS AND SCHOOL BOARD MEMBERS

Instead of "No Child Left Behind," the policy should be "No School Board Member Left Behind." The primary obligation of every superintendent is to educate each and every school board member. Doing so will make your job easier and make them look better. I would convince other school board members they should follow the relationship-building advice because anyone who has anything to do with education starts with the belief that things can get better, the culture can be better. If you and your school board feel better about the work you do, you will learn to interfere less with the classrooms where staff and students should always be valued. Few school boards were as publicly and openly dysfunctional as we once were, so I'm a believer. We are ordinary people who developed an extraordinary commitment to make it better. We did it by trusting each other, educating ourselves about the needs in the community, and by treating each other with respect. We were desperate for dignity, and there was no better feeling than being part of a respectable team that made schools a better place for students and staff.

—Janis Nowak
Taunton School Committee (2008–2011)

NOTES

Introduction

1. Gerry Tuoti, "School Committee Member Says Sorry for 'Hitler' Slur," *Taunton Daily Gazette*, July 24, 2007.
2. Ibid.
3. Malcolm Gladwell, *Outliers: The Stories of Success* (New York: Little, Brown and Company, 2008).
4. Joseph Marr Cronin, *Reforming Boston Schools, 1930 to the Present: Overcoming Corruption and Racial Segregation* (New York: Palgrave MacMillan, 2008), 3.
5. The United States Department of Commerce, June 10, 2014, http://www.census.gov/compendia/statab.
6. Eugene Aubrey Stratton, *Plymouth Colony, Its History & People: 1620–1691* (New York: Turner Publishing Company, 1988), 67.
7. William F. Hanna, *A History of Taunton Massachusetts* (Taunton, MA: Old Colony Historical Society, 2007), 4.
8. Ibid., 5.
9. Massachusetts Department of Elementary and Secondary Education, June 10, 2014, http://profiles.doe.mass.edu/.
10. Ibid.
11. Marilyn Halter, *Between Race and Ethnicity: Cape Verdean American Immigrants, 1860–1965* (Chicago: University of Illinois Press, 1993), 20.
12. United States Department of State, June 12, 2014, http://www.state.gov/p/af/ci/cv/.
13. Halter, *Between Race and Ethnicity.*
14. Richard Cross et al., "Beyond Demographic Destiny: An Analysis of Massachusetts Minority and White Student Achievement Gaps" (White paper, Pioneer Institute, Boston, MA, 2010).
15. Gerry Tuoti, "Despite Tight Budget, Taunton Schools Are Showing Results," *Taunton Daily Gazette*, September 29, 2013.

16. Massachusetts Department of Elementary and Secondary Education, June 10, 2014, http://www.doe.mass.edu/finance/.
17. Ronald Heifetz, *Leadership without Easy Answers* (Cambridge: President and Fellows of Harvard College, 1994), 2.

Chapter 1

1. John W. Gardner, *On Leadership* (New York: The Free Press, 1990), 3–12.
2. Yong Zhao, *Catching Up or Leading the Way: American Education in the Age of Globalization* (Alexandria, VA: ASCD, 2009).
3. Richard Parker, *John Kenneth Galbraith: His Life, His Politics, His Economics* (New York: Farrar, Straus and Giroux, 2005).
4. Stephanie Anderson and Jason A. Grissom, "Why Superintendents Turn Over," *American Educational Research Journal*, no. 6 (December 2012): 1146–1180.
5. Ibid.
6. Council of the Great City Schools, June 22, 2014, http://www.cgcs.org/cgcs.
7. Gerald L. Natkin et al., "Predicting and Modeling Superintendent Turnover," *Journal of School Leadership*, 13, no. 3 (May 2003): 328–346.
8. National School Boards Association, Superintendent Tenure: CUBE Survey Report (Alexandria, 2001), 5.
9. Council of the Great City Schools, *Urban School Superintendents: Characteristics, Tenure, and Salary* (Washington: Council of the Great City Schools, 2010).
10. Natkin, et al., "Predicting and Modeling Superintendent Turnover."
11. Anderson et al., "Why Superintendents Turn Over."
12. Ibid.
13. Ibid.
14. Ibid.
15. Michael G. Fullan and Suzanne Stiegelbauer, *The New Meaning of Educational Change* (New York, Teachers College Press, 1991).
16. Thomas L. Alsbury, "School Board Member and Superintendent Turnover and the Influence on Student Achievement: An Application of the Dissatisfaction Theory," *Leadership and Policy in Schools* (2008): 202–229.
17. Anderson et al., "Why Superintendents Turn Over."
18. Larry Cuban, *The Managerial Imperative and the Practice of Leadership in Schools* (Albany: State University of New York Press, 1988); Susan Moore Johnson, *Leading to Change: The Challenge of the New Superintendency* (San Francisco: Jossey-Bass Inc., 1996).
19. United States Department of Education. National Commission on Excellence in Education. *A Nation at Risk: The Imperative for Educational Reform* (Washington: GPO, 1983).
20. Sean F. Reardon, "The Widening Income Achievement Gap," *Educational Leadership* (2013): 10–16.

21. National Center for Educational Statistics, June 30, 2014, http://nces.ed.gov/nationsreportcard/.
22. Thomas E. Glass, Lars Bjork, and Cryss C. Brunner, *The Study of the American Superintendency, 2000: A Look at the Superintendent of Education in the New Millennium* (Arlington: AASA, 2000).
23. Harvard Graduate School of Education, June 30, 2014, https://www.gse.harvard.edu/news/13/05/alonso-named-professor-practice.
24. Paul Reide, "Tough-Minded at the Helm of Charm City," *School Administrator* 69, no. 2 (February, 2012): 51.
25. New York City Department of Education, November 9, 2014, http://schools.nyc.gov/AboutUs/default.htm.
26. Andres Alonso, in discussion with the author, 2014.
27. Thomas E. Wilcox, Diane Bell-McKoy, and Laura Gamble, "Six Steps for Post-Alonso School Progress," *Baltimore Sun Chronicle,* May 13, 2013.
28. Harvard Graduate School of Education, June 30, 2014, https://www.gse.harvard.edu/news/13/05/alonso-named-professor-practice.
29. Iowa Association of School Boards, "The Lighthouse Inquiry: School Board/Superintendent Team Behaviors in School Districts with Extreme Differences in Student Achievement," *American Educational Research Association Annual Meeting,* (2001): 1–62.
30. Moore Johnson, *Leading to Change*; Glass et al., *The Study of the American Superintendency, 2000.*
31. Iowa Association of School Boards. "The Lighthouse Inquiry"; Susan J. Rosenholtz, *Teachers' Workplace: The Social Organization of Schools* (White Plains, NY: Longman, Inc., 1989).
32. Iowa Association of School Boards. "The Lighthouse Inquiry."
33. Iowa Association of School Boards. "The Lighthouse Inquiry."
34. Glass et al., *The Study of the American Superintendency, 2000.*
35. Rosabeth Moss Kanter, "Transforming Giants," *Harvard Business Review* (2008): 43–52.

Chapter 2

1. Barry C. Jentz and Jerome T. Murphy, "Starting Confused: How Leaders Start When They Don't Know Where to Start," *Phi Delta Kappan* (2005): 736–746.
2. Ibid.

Chapter 4

1. Lucius Annaeus Seneca, 4 BC–65 AD.
2. Stacey Childress et al., eds. *Managing School Districts for High Performance: Cases in Public Education Leadership* (Cambridge: Harvard Education Press, 2007).
3. Richard F. Elmore, "Teaching, Learning, and Organization: School Restructuring and the Recurring Dilemmas of Reform" (paper presented at the annual meeting of the American Educational Research Association, Chicago, IL, 1991).

4. Thomas E. Glass, Lars Bjork, and Cryss C. Brunner, *The Study of the American Superintendency, 2000: A Look at the Superintendent of Education in the New Millennium* (Arlington: AASA, 2000).
5. Nancy D. Olsen and Howard W. Olsen, "Elements of a Strategic Plan," *National Association of Church Business Administration* (2009): 23.

Chapter 5

1. We began using this inclusive goal-setting process in the Taunton Public Schools in 2010. In 2012, Massachusetts adopted a similar process for all educators in the Commonwealth.

2. George Doran, Arthur Miller, and James Cunningham, "There's a S.M.A.R.T. Way to Write Management's Goals and Objectives," *Management Review* 70, no. 11 (November 1981): 35–36.

Chapter 7

1. Terrance E. Deal and Kent D. Peterson, *Shaping School Culture: The Heart of Leadership* (San Francisco: Jossey-Bass, 1999).
2. Massachusetts Association for School Superintendents, August 28, 2014, http://www.massupt.org/pages/MASS.
3. Susan M. Cover, "Maine House: School Superintendents Can Live Anywhere," *Portland Press Herald* April 4, 2013. http://www.pressherald.com/2013/04/04/vote-backs-local-residency-control-_2013-04-05/.

Chapter 8

1. National School Public Relations, *How Strong Communications Help Superintendents Get and Keep Their Jobs* (Rockville: National School Public Relations Association, 2007).
2. Harris, Alma, Christopher Day, David Hopkins, Mark Hadfield, Andy Hargreaves, and Christopher Chapman. *Effective leadership for school improvement*. Routledge, 2013.
3. Richard Elmore, *Building a New Structure for School Leadership* (Washington, DC: The Albert Shanker Institute, 2000).
4. Kowalski, Theodore J., Robert S. McCord, George J. Peterson, Phillip I. Young, and Noelle M. Ellerson. *The American school superintendent: 2010 decennial study*. R&L Education, 2011.

Chapter 9

1. Urban Dictionary, September 17, 2014, http://www.urbandictionary.com.
2. John Blaydes, *The Educator's Book of Quotes* (Thousand Oaks: Corwin Press, Inc., 2003), 144.
3. Barbara L. Brock and Marilyn L. Grady, *The Daily Practices of Successful Principals* (Thousand Oaks: Corwin Press, Inc., 2012), 46.

ACKNOWLEDGMENTS

THIS BOOK IS ABOUT RELATIONSHIPS, so it seems fitting for me to recognize those who are the most important in my life. First, to my husband and my family, the most treasured of all my relationships, thank you for putting up with me and the "motherboard" (the giant, oversized laptop I dragged along everywhere) while I worked on this project—you make me proud every day. To "my second family," my school board and my school community members past and present, I am forever inspired by your belief in public education and children. Finally, to two of my most cherished teachers, Dr. Gordon Donaldson and the late Dr. Dave Brown, you taught me by word and by deed that job one for any school leader is to build strong relationships. You made me work harder, do better, and want more for myself. I owe every good thing that I manage to accomplish on behalf of my students to all of these special people in my life.

I also owe a debt of gratitude to the Harvard Education Publishing Group and Nancy Walser, my editor and the author of *The Essential School Board Book,* without whom this book never would have been written. A heartfelt thank you for believing in me.

ABOUT THE AUTHOR

JULIE HACKETT has been a public educator since 1992, and her background includes experience at the elementary, middle, high school, and post-secondary levels. She began her career as a high school English teacher in Maine, where she was a passionate advocate for helping struggling students learn to read. Julie became a frequent presenter on this topic, sharing ways to engage all learners. As a member of the National Writing Project and an active teacher researcher, she developed an innovative program and partnership between preschool students and her struggling high school readers. In 2000, her efforts culminated in a book, called *Strategic Reading: Guiding Students to Lifelong Literacy, 6–12* published by Heinemann, that she coauthored with Tanya Baker and Jeffrey Wilhelm.

After being promoted to the position of Dean of Students, Julie served as an elementary/middle school principal in a regional school system in Maine. In 2001, she was appointed to the Maine Learning Technology Initiative (MLTI)—the single largest 1:1 educational technology program in the world, designed to put technology in the hands of every middle school student in the state. At this time, she pursued a doctoral degree in educational leadership, which she earned in 2005 after completing her dissertation titled "Exploring the Links among Professional Development, Teacher Performance and Student Achievement."

Julie then began her career as a central office administrator in 2002, when she was appointed to the position of Director of Curriculum, Instruction, and Assessment, a role she held in two different school systems in Maine. She led both districts in strategic planning and the creation of comprehensive teacher-developed local assessment systems. In addition, she taught graduate-level courses at her alma mater, the University of Maine, including an instructional leadership course for aspiring principals and a series of gifted and talented courses that she developed for educators. In 2007, Julie and her husband, Frank, and their children, Parker, Cameron, and Kelsey, moved to Massachusetts. She first served as Assistant Superintendent in Taunton, and then Deputy Superintendent of Teaching and Learning in Brookline, where she also led the strategic planning work, as well as efforts to close achievement gaps.

In 2009, Julie became the first female superintendent in Taunton, Massachusetts. One of twenty-four urban school districts in the Commonwealth, the Taunton Public Schools is a diverse school community with approximately eight thousand two hundred students and one thousand two hundred fifty employees. The district had been consistently in the bottom 10 to 12 percent for per pupil expenditures, receiving the least amount of funding of any urban school system in the state for several years running; despite this, its student achievement indicators across a variety of disciplines rivaled those of other high-achieving, affluent urban districts in Massachusetts with per pupil expenditures more than doubling those of the Taunton Public Schools. Julie and her team found creative ways to implement and fund a districtwide model of inclusion that is one of the first in the state, and expand wrap-around services, the arts, foreign languages, and career and technical education offerings. These efforts led to the lowest dropout rates (less than 1 percent) and highest graduation rates (90 percent) in the school system's history. Julie also takes pride in her work as a mentor, helping at-risk high school students graduate and go on to college.

In her career as a central office administrator, Julie has worked with five school boards and more than thirty school board members. She has been an invited guest speaker at state and national conferences where she has shared strategies for establishing effective superintendent and school board relations. Now in her sixth year as superintendent, Julie Hackett and her school board have worked together to transform their schools and build superintendent–school board relationships focused on their mission of "academic excellence for every student, every classroom, and every school."

INDEX